Principled Productivity

This book demonstrates that ethical treatment of everyone in an organization:

1. Will increase productivity in all the functional activities of the organization as well as its members.
2. Will ensure the growth of the organization as a result of continuous improvements that may have been initiated by management but will be continuously improved due to motivated employees.

It achieves this by:

1. The presentation of examples from personal experience and a review of the literature.
2. Providing a list of critical questions for each function whose correct solutions will provide a metric that enables and establishes obtainable goals for improvement.

This book is unique because it requires the decision-maker to examine each potential decision and ask the questions:

1. Do alternative methods exist that will achieve the desired goals, which will minimize the long-term adverse effects on affected employees and the future viability of the organization?
2. When is the appropriate time to implement this decision?
3. What is the best way to implement this decision?

The decision may involve a reduction in force (RIF), a potential change in a vendor or a manufacturing process, the formation of a safety team, and/or the installation or modification of an incentive system. The decisions could be involved in manufacturing, logistics, quality, or healthcare. This work will benefit everyone in leadership positions in all branches of government, manufacturing, logistics, human relations, and healthcare, especially those working with frontline employees, staff and customers.

Principled Productivity

Why Ethical Treatment of Everyone in an Organization Will Result in Increased Productivity

Gerald J. Watson Jr.

Routledge
Taylor & Francis Group

A PRODUCTIVITY PRESS BOOK

First published 2023
by Routledge
605 Third Avenue, New York, NY 10158

and by Routledge
4 Park Square, Milton Park, Abingdon, Oxon, OX14 4RN

Routledge is an imprint of the Taylor & Francis Group, an informa business

ISBN: 978-1-032-29842-9 (hbk)
ISBN: 978-1-032-29841-2 (pbk)
ISBN: 978-1-003-30230-8 (ebk)

DOI: 10.4324/9781003302308

Typeset in Garamond
by Deanta Global Publishing Services, Chennai, India

I want to recognize the positive impact of a person for whom I was privileged to work for 10 years. This person shaped my current philosophy of interaction with customers, vendors, suppliers, and employees. This person taught me the value of honesty, respect, and integrity not just in the workplace but in the everyday world. To him, these were not just words but standards by which he lived his life. These values were much more important than money and material things since I have heard him say on many occasions that you can always get more money but once you lose respect, honesty, and integrity, you can never retrieve these. This person was the late Robert Gibbon Pender of Marietta, GA.

Contents

List of Figures

List of Tables

Foreword

I was surprised and pleased to hear from Jerry Watson recently. His e-mail renewed a relationship that began some 50 years ago when we were coworkers at Star Paper Tube, then a privately owned paper converting company operating in the Southeastern US. After a little "catching up", Jerry asked me to write a foreword message to be included in his new book. I was flattered and certainly am willing to accommodate his request.

I remember Jerry as a hardworking and effective Industrial Engineer. In my role as Controller, we worked on many projects aimed at improving efficiency and reducing costs. Jerry was effective because he asked a lot of questions and communicated well with our employees and vendors. Jerry's "gift of gab", listening skills, and concern for others led to the implementation of successful changes in our company and to his being held in high regard by our fellow workers.

Our time together as coworkers ended in 1984. Since that time Jerry has continued his work career and education, achieving a PhD in Industrial Engineering at North Carolina A&T in Greensboro, NC. Jerry has used this background and work experience to expand his career into the world of teaching at the college level.

"Professor" or "Dr." Watson just seems a good fit!

Jerry has my best wishes and respect as he authors this new book documenting our shared belief in the positive effects of honesty, accuracy, and ethical relationships in the workplace.

Fred E. Garrison
Controller and Treasurer
Star Paper Tube, Inc.

Preface

This work is a follow-up to two previous ones by this author. The first one – *Critical Thinking: Learning from Mistakes and How to Prevent Them* – categorizes the causes of mistakes committed and observed by the author to develop a format that employs the use of critical thinking to prevent or at the very least minimize the losses that could result from the commission of a mistake. The book recognizes the axiom that we, as human beings, make mistakes and demonstrates with examples the effect that employment of critical thinking can have on reducing the frequency and severity of mistakes. The book emphasizes that one of the most important critical questions is best stated as "Murphy's Law – what is the worst that can happen?" The importance of addressing this question quickly to seek a long term solution to is based on his numerous years of experience of the author during his professional career in manufacturing, healthcare, federal and county government and education.

The second book titled *Integration of Methods Improvement and Measurement into Industrial Engineering Functions* emphasizes that these techniques form the foundation of all industrial engineering applications. The goal of industrial engineering as defined by the Bureau of Labor statistics is to "determine the most effective ways to use the basic factors of production, e.g., people, machines, materials, information, and energy to make a product or provide a service" [1].

The focus of industrial engineers is to seek continual cost-effective improvements in productivity, reductions in the accident and incident rations, increased throughput, and a reduced level of raw material, work in process, and finished goods inventory. All of these goals are achievable as a result of improvement in the factors of the manufacturing, service, and healthcare industries. Similar to a GPS system that enables travelers to arrive at their destinations in a timely manner from the beginning point of their journey, these two tools provide the industrial engineer not only a starting point but a methodology for continuous improvement.

This work discusses the application of these tools to a majority of situations with which industrial engineers are confronted. This text begins with the definition of a method and an explanation of various tools that can be used to effect improvement. Implied in the definition is a methodology for measurement to enable before-and-after comparisons. This measurement methodology must be simple, easy to use and understand, and most importantly produce consistent results. The text then discusses the application of these two techniques to various situations.

The goal of this last work is to ensure that the efforts consumed in the use of critical thinking to ask questions result in the reduction of human mistakes and to ensure the improvements achieved as a result of the application of the basic tools of industrial engineering: measurement and methods improvement. If the appropriate questions are asked and the basic tools are properly applied, these changes will be the stimulus for future changes over time regardless of the changes in technology or personnel.

Based on the experience and observations of the author, the probability of this occurring will increase if the following occurs:

The decision-maker employs critical thinking to:

1. Ensure that all physical assets that the decision affects are treated ethically.

These assets include employees, equipment, physical and all resources, including those that occur naturally and artificially.

2. Ensure that long-term benefits receive maximum priority over short-term benefits. These long-term benefits must also include the global effects of these decisions. Not all of these benefits are quantifiable as the elimination of lead in paint and gasoline but represent actions that are the right thing to do.
3. Ensure that everyone involved in the decision-making process understands that decision-making is a compromise between two or more parties and that long-term results can only be achieved if all parties derive equal benefits from the decision.

Reference

1. Flitter, T. (2011). What is an industrial engineer? Retrieved 8/5/2022 from: https://www.iiela.org/what-is-an-industrial-engineer/

Acknowledgments

I want to acknowledge the positive impact that various people have had on my life. These people have appeared at the right time for the right reason. These people include my wife of too many years to count, my daughter, my parents, my drill sergeant at Ft Bragg, and students and faculty over the many years as an instructor that taught me how to be a better person and educator.

My Motivation

I wrote this book to achieve three goals:

1. To acknowledge the transformations that I have observed that have occurred over time concerning both personal and business relationships.
2. To effect change in these relationships that will result in an increase in honesty and respect for others during the decision-making process.
3. To present examples from experience that demonstrate that decisions can be made and executed that reflect a win–win situation for both the decision-maker and those affected by the decision.

Example A

During the first few years of the Vietnam War, family members were notified of casualties by telegram. This method achieved its goal but in a very detached personal manner. This was changed later to a policy that members of casualties were notified in person usually by a team of at least two members of the military. The team, usually an officer and a non-commissioned officer, provided the family members with details concerning the loss, if asked by family members, and the next steps that would be taken by the military to give appropriate recognition to the family for their loss.

I made a notification to one such family. The results were the same – the family suffered a loss, but the difference was that the family was treated with respect.

Example B

I purchased a material handling system for a plant located in the Southeast from a company located in the Midwest for $65K in 1976. Detailed specifications for the equipment were provided to the authors company. As the author shook the hand of the company representative, he looked the representative in the eye confirming the verbal agreement between the two companies. After several unsuccessful attempts were made to use the system as designed and the realization that future efforts would be unproductive, I decided to disassemble the equipment and return it to the contractor. No money was exchanged. After receipt of the equipment, I received a letter from the contractor expressing regret that the system did not perform as needed.

During this entire process, each company maintained an honest, transparent, and respectful relationship.

Example C

During my professional career, I have been laid off from my position twice. The first layoff happened after I had been promoted and received numerous verbal positive comments. In fact, I relocated my family to accept this position. After working there for almost three years, I was summoned to the office of my boss while taking a physical inventory at approximately 6:30 pm on New Year's Eve and was told that it was in the best interest of this company that I was no longer employed there. I was given a check for the period worked, which included an amount for unused vacation. I asked for the reason of my sudden termination and was told that providing a reason was not required by law and that I would not be given one. The loss of my job with health insurance benefits was emotionally and financially devastating since at the time my wife was working part-time and we had a young child. Overcoming this loss required many therapy sessions.

The second occurred while working for a company that had experienced a 50 percent reduction in sales over the last few years. I was summoned to the controller's office on a Tuesday morning and was advised that due to the loss of sales, expenses needed to be reduced. I was told that my salary and benefits would continue for the next 13 weeks. I was further advised that my work performance was excellent and that they would provide a positive referral if asked.

The result of both decisions was the same – the loss of my current job. The difference is the circumstances associated with each decision. The first treated me with no respect for me or my family. My family and I were treated like a piece of non-recyclable trash. The second treated me and my family with respect and dignity. I did not like losing my job, but at least I understood the reason and was given financial and emotional support, which enabled me to pursue other opportunities with a positive attitude.

The point of these comparisons is to illustrate that each decision can result in a win–win or win–lose situation. The first was a win for the company and a loss for me and my family that resulted in both financial and mental hardships. The second was a win–win, a short-term win for the company and a long-term win for me. For the company it was a win since expenses were better aligned with revenue and a long-term win for me and my family since I was able to move forward in a positive manner. After the loss of that job, I was able to gain a research and teaching position at a university with new learning and travel opportunities.

About the Author

Dr. Gerald J. Watson, Jr. earned B.S. and M.S. degrees in Industrial Management from the Georgia Institute of Technology, was commissioned and spent two years in the U.S. Army with the last tour in Vietnam. He returned to school to earn a Ph.D. degree in Industrial Engineering from North Carolina A&T State University in 2009 after working as a manufacturing engineer/manager and safety manager for various companies and consultant for over thirty years. His teaching experience includes the community college and the university level for over twenty years. He retired from the Department of Applied Engineering Technology at North Carolina A&T State University in 2019. He is the author of two books; *Critical Thinking: Learning from Mistakes, How to Prevent Them* and *Integration of Methods Improvement and Measurement into Industrial Engineering Functions.* He also co-authored a text with a former colleague at NC A&T, Dr. Aixi Chout, *Applied Engineering Design* and ten papers at various conference proceedings. His research interests include the reshoring of manufacturing and the application of the sub-optimal theory of Dr. John Nash of Princeton to real world applications.

About the Author

About the Illustrator

Jesse Derouin has worked for over ten years accumulating valuable industry experience. Jesse has had the benefit of having worked in several capacities gaining an understanding of how to successfully combine people, equipment, and processes to create favorable outcomes. As an adult returning student, he set about achieving an undergraduate degree in engineering, where he met Dr. Watson. He is now a graduate student studying for his advanced engineering degree in sustainable design.

Introduction

This book will demonstrate that productivity is inversely related to the ethical treatment of employees, equipment used in the production and distribution of products and services, vendors, customers, and regulatory agencies. It will achieve this goal through the presentation and discussion of numerous examples from personal experience and peer-reviewed studies from the literature.

The author is an industrial engineer with over 40 years of experience in manufacturing, healthcare, supply chain, logistics, and education. He has worked for a number and variety of companies in different industries as a full-time employee and as a consultant. He has taught at both the community college and university levels for over 20 years both part and full time; returned to school after working over 30 years to earn a PhD in Industrial and Systems Engineering; has served his country as a lieutenant in the Army for two years with both stateside and overseas (Viet Nam) assignments.

He has taught a number of different courses with varying subject material, but his focus as an instructor was the use of critical thinking to enable students to better understand the subject and to employ that understanding to effect improvements. He also emphasized teamwork, and oral and written communication skills using assigned projects and written assignments.

As a result of easily preventable mistakes made and observed during his career, he has learned to ask critical questions prior to the initiation of a project, which focus on the need for and benefits of the project and the long-term sustainability and continuous improvement opportunities.

The purposes of this work are:

1. To validate the importance of the numerous key productivity indices (KPIs) such as productivity, efficiency, downtime percent, cost of quality (COQ), employee turnover rate, inventory turnover rate, accident and

incident rates, etc., including their meaning, calculation, applications, and the factors that can result in achieving less than optimum.

2. To challenge potential decision-makers to develop a list of critical questions that will result in:

   i. The maximum net sustainable long-term benefits for employees, the equipment used in the production and distribution of goods and services, vendors, customers, regulatory agencies, and the environment.

   ii. A reduction in the probability of making a mistake that will create more liabilities for the company than the benefits that the correct decision will generate.

   iii. The acknowledgment that Murphy's law "What is the worst that can happen?" applies and that the honest answer is one that yields positive net benefits.

   iv. Adherence to the policy of "First do no harm", a saying in Latin that is used primarily in the health field but not included in the original or modern versions of the Hippocratic Oath. The meaning of this phrase is that it is often better to do nothing rather than take action that can result in more harm [1].

3. To ensure that everyone acknowledges and adheres to the axiom that the value and utility of decisions are directly related to the accuracy, reliability, and reproducibility of the information on which the decision is based.

4. To change the paradigm in the decision-making process to ensure that every decision incorporates the ethical treatment of employees, the equipment used in the production and distribution of goods and services, vendors, regulatory agencies, the environment, and all others with which the organization interacts. This change will occur as the result of the development of a framework that will require all decision-makers to ensure that all decisions are made ethically. It achieves this by defining ethical leadership and the role that ethical leadership has in leading the organization to seek and conduct all its transactions ethically which is critical to the long-term success of the organization. The goal is to obtain a consensus decision so that it is a win-win situation, a win for various parties involved and the employee's long-term win for the organization. Critical thinking will be employed to generate a list of questions that will form a framework that will combine critical thinking with a win-win strategy [2]. A win-win strategy is a type of suboptimal one in which there is no winner-take-all strategy.

In a previous text, one author concluded based on mistakes that he had made or witnessed that over 80% had resulted from the failure of the decision-maker to take an additional step prior to making and executing a decision. This can be seen in Table I.1.

These results can be seen graphically in Figure I.1.

The final step in this framework requires the decision-maker to ask himself the question: "How can this decision be made so that it is a win-win

Table I.1 Distribution of Errors by Cause

Reasons for Failures	Percentage of Errors	Number of Errors
Failure to consider all aspects of the project	36.4	12
Failure to ask others for assistance	27.3	9
Failure to consider all costs of operation	18.2	6
In a hurry	15.1	5
To meet a deadline	3.0	1
Total of all mistakes	100.0	33

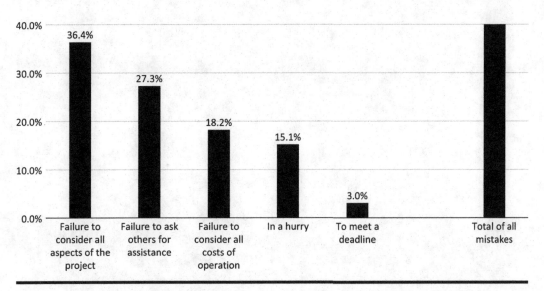

Figure I.1 Frequency distribution of author-committed and -observed mistakes committed [3].

situation, a win for the various parties involved and a long-term win for the organization?" This framework will focus on determining the best suboptimal solution that yields the maximum benefits for the organization while generating the least detrimental results to all affected parties. Emphasis will be on the solution and not the timing of the solution.

5. To demonstrate with examples from personal experience and literature the inverse relationship between the ethical treatment of employees, the equipment used in the production and distribution of goods and services, customers, vendors, etc., and increased KPI.

References

1. Gill, N.S. (2021, February 16). Is 'first do no harm' part of the hippocratic oath? Retrieved 11/5/2022 from: https://www.thoughtco.com/first-do-no-harm -hippocratic-oath-118780
2. What is a win-win situation? Definition and tips. Retrieved 9/18/2022 from: indeed.com/careIer-advice/career-development/win-win-situations#:~:text=A%2 0win-win%20situation%20is%20a%20resolution%20to%20a,in%20both%20 parties%20voluntarily%20accepting%20the%20proposed%20solution
3. Watson, G.J., and Derouin, J.J. (2021). *Critical Thinking- Learning from Mistakes and How to Prevent Them*. CRC Press, Boca Raton, FL, ISBN-978–0-367-35460-2

Chapter 1

Business Ethics

1.1 What Is Business Ethics?

Business Ethics has been defined as the collection of moral principles, values, and policies that oversee the manner in which organizations and individuals participate in various activities. The subject matter of business ethics includes areas that have the potential of being confrontational as discrimination, insider trading, bribery, social responsibility, etc. Often laws have been passed to provide guidelines for organizations to follow [1].

Another definition is the study of the mechanisms by which organizations can conduct themselves that will ethically improve society. Areas such as trade, effective altruism, exploitation, incentives for good behavior, and compensation for employees are included [2].

1.2 What Is the Origin of Business Ethics?

The concept can be traced to the 1960s of the twentieth century due to the increasing concerns that society had for the environment, the society in general, and corporate responsibility. The goal was to ensure that everyone was treated fairly [3].

A. What are some examples of unethical but legal actions?
1. Sharing of your letter of resignation to fellow employees.
2. Hiring someone for a position that was not advertised.
3. Sharing your salary with other employees.
4. Hiring a relative instead of an unrelated potential employee.

DOI: 10.4324/9781003302308-1

5. Terminating employees via email.
6. Using a random employee to inform you of your termination [4].

1.3 What Laws Exist to Prevent or Reduce the Potential of Illegal Behavior?

In response to several financial scandalsin 2002, Congress passed the Sarbanes-Oxley (SOX) Act. It was named for its two sponsors, Sen. Paul S. Sarbanes (D-Md.) and Rep. Michael G. Oxley (R-Ohio).

The Sarbanes-Oxley Act, abbreviated as SOX, was passed in 2002, was named after its sponsors, Senator Paul S. Sarbanes (D-MD) and Rep. Michael G. Oxley (R-OH), makes it more difficult for corporations to commit financial fraud, protecting investors. It states that all CFOs and CEOs of publicly traded American companies must sign a statement that they have read the reports (annual and quarterly), and vouch that they are accurate. Additionally, businesses must explain the logic if they don't have an ethics code. It also created the Public Company Accounting Oversight Board [5].

Involved in these scandals included publicly traded companies such as Enron, WorldCom, Tyco International, Theranos, U.S. Bank, and Dollar General.

Various laws have been passed to prevent discrimination in the workplace. The Fair Labor Standards Act established the basis concerning fairness in hours and wages. The Civil Rights Act passed in 1964 is the foundation that prevents discrimination in the workplace. The Age Discrimination Act passed in 1967 addresses the discrimination that older workers face in the workplace. This act was passed since age discrimination was not included in the Civil Rights Act of 1964 [6].

In 1970, the Occupational Safety and Health Act (OSHA) was passed to ensure that employees had safe and healthful working conditions. The Act established standards that were enforced with fines and penalties. The Act also worked for improvement by establishing various training programs, education, and assistance [7].

Numerous other laws exist including the prevention of law enforcement conduct, laws to prevent sexual misconduct, laws to enforce traffic rules, etc.

1.4 Why Have Business Ethics Changed over Time?

The late 1800s was a time when the economy of the US realized a drastic change. Huge companies existed and were presided over by industrial barons. Examples include J.P. Morgan whose empire was finance, John Jay Astor who specialized in real estate, and the Vanderbilts who controlled the railroads. These industrial barons had a sizable influence on the economy and, as a result, possessed a tremendous amount of influence in the federal government, so much so that it was thought that big interests corrupted the federal government. The initial reaction of Vanderbilt, when faced with the concept of operating a railroad for the benefit of the public, was "The public be damned" [8].

Ethical standards do not remain fixed; they transform in response to evolving situations. Over time, people change, technology advances, and cultural mores (i.e., acquired culture and manners) shift. What was considered an appropriate or accepted business practice 100 or even 50 years ago may not carry the same moral weight it once did. However, this does not mean ethics and moral behavior are relative. It simply acknowledges that attitudes change in relationship to historical events and that cultural perspective and the process of acculturation are not stagnant.

Ethics is not static but changes in each new era. Technology is a driving force in ethical shifts, as can be seen in tracing changes from the age of mercantilism to the Industrial Revolution to the postindustrial era and the [9] Information Age. Some of the most successful recent efforts to advance ethical practices have come from influences outside the industry, including government regulation and consumer pressure [10].

1.5 What Are Some Examples of Illegal Behavior?

1.5.1 Enron

Contributors to the corruption of Enron include their banker, Merrill Lynch; their auditor, Arthur Anderson; and attorneys for Enron due to partiality to Enron. For example, Merrill Lynch contributed by assisting Enron in the sale of oil barges to Nigeria, enabling Enron to attain its target goal of $12 million; The demise of Enron can be attributed to the unethical behavior of the accounting firm of Arthur Anderson and its team of attorneys. The contribution of Arthur Anderson was the failure to adhere to the ethical practices required by its profession and the failure of its team f attorneys who failed to oppose fraudulent activities [11].

1.5.2 WorldCom

The demise of WorldCom was due to the fraudulent capitalizing of expenses. The company was found guilty in the United States Securities and Exchange Commission (SEC) investigation of various methods to cook its books by some expenses as capital expenditures rather than normal expenses to enable WorldCom to incorrectly increase profit and the use of fake accounting entries to promote the concept that it was a thriving enterprise. WorldCom admitted to inflating earnings by almost $4 billion in 2002. The demise of WorldCom resulted in the loss of almost 30,000 jobs and billions in retirement accounts. WorldCom changed its name to MCI as a result of a class action lawsuit brought by employees of nearly $51 million. The perpetrators of this fraud, Bernard Ebbers, the CEO, and Scott Sullivan, the CFO, were charged with financial fraud and both served prison terms. The auditor for WorldCom was Arthur Anderson [12].

1.5.3 Tyco International

The Tyco scandal resulted from the theft by CEO Chairman Dennis Kozlowski and Mark Swartz, the previous CFO, of stealing as much as $600 million from the company. The two were charged in the second trial, since the first trial resulted in a mistrial, and sentenced to a maximum of 25 years in prison. In addition, the shareholders received $2.92 billion as a result of a class action lawsuit. The auditing firm PricewaterhouseCoopers paid $225 million to affected investors [13].

1.5.4 Theranos

Another example is that of Theranos Inc., a consumer healthcare technology start-up. It was founded in 2003 by then 19-year-old Ms. Elizabeth Holmes (Founder and CEO). The name Theranos is a combination of the words "therapy" and "diagnosis".

The company claimed that with only a small sample of blood, it could perform numerous blood tests accurately and quickly. Ms. Holmes raised over $700 million from venture capitalists and private investors and had a value of $10 billion. The company failed to demonstrate its new technology, and as a result, the company was dissolved in 2018 due to litigation and sanctions from the Centers for Medicare and Medicaid Services (WCG FDA news 2016).

In January 2022, Ms. Holmes was found guilty on 4 out of 11 fraud charges with which she was charged. She was sentenced to more than eleven years in prison [14]. Tamesh Balwani,the former company President, was tried and found guilty of twelve counts of of fraud and sentenced to almost thirteen years in prison [15].

1.5.5 *U.S. Bank*

U.S. Bank, the fifth largest US commercial bank, was fined for the illegal acquisition of customer credit, reposts, and the opening of accounts without the permission of customers. The Minneapolis bank applied pressure on employees to meet sales goals through the proposal of incentives for the sales of various bank products. To achieve these goals employees illegally obtained credit reports and personal information to open accounts without the consent of the customers. The bank was fined $37.5 million by the Consumer Financial Protection Bureau [16].

1.5.6 *Dollar General*

Dollar General received another fine of $1.6 million from OSHA for violation of worker safety regulations. These fines resulted from visits by inspectors in four different locations. These fines represent part of the overall fines that exceed $9.6 million resulting from these inspections. The fines resulted from exposing employees to hazardous working conditions, repeated violations for the failure to install and label fire extinguishers, the failure to maintain exit routes, the failure to keep electric panels unobstructed and clear to allow access, and having a locked exit door that required a key [17].

References

1. Twin, A. (2022). Ethics: Definition, principles, why they're important. *Investopedia-Business*. Retrieved 5/22/2022 from: https://www.investopedia.com/terms/b/business-ethics.asp#:~:text=The%20concept%20of%20business%20ethics%20began%20in%20the,period%2C%20the%20concept%20of%20business%20ethics%20has%20evolved
2. What is business ethics. (n.d.). GeorgeTown University, McDonough of business. Retrieved 8/11/2022 from: https://gisme.georgetown.edu/what-is-business-ethics/
3. Twin, A. (2022). Business ethics: Definition, principles, why they're important. Retrived 6/22/2022 from: https://www.investopedia.com/terms/b/business-ethics.asp#:~:text=The%20concept%20of%20business%20ethics%20began%20in%20the,period%2C%20the%20concept%20of%20business%20ethics%20has%20evolved
4. Marshall, J. (2013). Workplace ethics: 62 Things that are legal, but 22 of them are unethical. Retrieved 7/11/2022 from: https://ethicsalarms.com/2013/11/05/workplace-ethics-62-things-that-are-legal-but-22-of-them-are-unethical/

5. What is the Sarbanes-Oxley (SOX) Act of 2002? *Investopedia*. Retrieved 9/30, 2022 from: https://www.bing.com/search?q=purpose%20of%20the%20 Sarbanes-Oxley%20Act%20in%202002.&form=SWAUA2

6. Other laws preventing discrimination. (n.d.). The lawyers and jurists. Received 8/1/2022 from: https://www.lawyersnjurists.com/article/other-laws-preventing -discrimination

7. About OSHA. (n.d.). Occupational Safety and Health Administration. U. S. Department of Labor. Retrieved 8/11/2022 from: https://www.osha.gov /aboutosha

8. Gordon, J.S. (1989). The public be damned. *The Business of America*. September/October 1989;40(6). Retrieved 8/15/2022 from: https://www .americanheritage.com/public-be-damned

9. Business. (2020). What is ethical leadership? Western Governors University. Retrieved 6/11/2022 from: https://www.wgu.edu/blog/what-is-ethical -leadership2001.html

10. Resnick, D.B. (2020). What is ethnics in research and why it is important? Retrieved 8/2/2022 from: https://www.niehs.nih.gov/research/resources /bioethics/whatis/index.cfm

11. Pratap (2016). Contribution of Enrons's bankers, auditors and attorneys to its demise, Notesmatic. Retrieved 3/15/2022 from: https://notesmatic.com /contribution-enrons-bankers-auditors-attorneys-demise/#:~:text=The%20 auditors%20working%20for%20Enron%20were%20Arthur%20Anderson,it %20had%20a%20major%20involvement%20in%20the%20scandal

12. The WorldCom scandal: A simple scan missed by auditors. *Zero Theft Movement*. Retrieved 4/11/2022 from: https://zerotheft.net/the-worldcom -scandal-a-simple-scam-missed-by-auditors/

13. What was the Tyco International scandal. (n.d.). *The Thomas Herold in Economics, Laws and Regulations*. Retrieved 3/11/2022 from: https://www .financial-dictionary.info/terms/tyco-international-scandal/

14. Trial of Elizabeth Holmes. Retrieved 3/18/2023. https://www.nytimes.com /news-event/elizabeth-holmes-theranos-trial

15. https://www.cnn.com/2022/12/07/tech/sunny-balwani-theranos-trial -sentencing/index.html

16. Maruf, R. (2022). U.S. Bank fined for opening 'sham' accounts for customers, *CNN*. Retrieved 6/22/2022 from: https://www.cnn.com/2022/07/30/business/us -bank-cfbp-fine/index.html#:~:text=The%20CFBP%20announced%20Thursday %20that%20it%20fined%20U.S.,CFPB%20Director%20Rohit%20Chopra%20in %20a%20press%20release

17. Staff Writers (2022). Dollar General fined over 1.6 million for worker safety violations. *Insurance Journal*. Retrieved 5/11/2022 from: https://www .insurancejournal.com/news/southeast/2022/11/03/693198.htm

Chapter 2

Ethical Leadership

2.1 What Is Ethical Leadership?

Ethical leadership has been defined as "leadership demonstrating and promoting normatively appropriate conduct through personal actions and interpersonal relations" [1].

It is a type of leadership:

1. In which the leaders possess the ability to guide individuals in various decisions involving ethical values such as fairness, morals, honesty, equality, and respect.
2. That teaches the difference between right and wrong.

A simple difference between the selection of right and wrong behavior can be summarized as:

Performing the right behavior is one that complies with current laws, justice, and morality, whereas not performing the wrong thing does not comply with current laws, justice, and morality.

a. The right behavior is defined as the one that is appropriate, is proper, and fits the current situation, whereas the wrong behavior is not appropriate, is improper, and does not fit the current situation.
b. The origin of both words is Latin: the right was derived from the Latin word "rectus", which is translated as "straight"; the wrong way is derived from the Latin word "pravus", which when translated means "crooked" [2].

DOI: 10.4324/9781003302308-2

Ethical behavior is critical to improving the morale of employees to reduce the likelihood of unethical behavior for additional gain.

This type of leadership is guided by these major tenets:

1. Fairness which reflects the manner others should be treated and how one expects to be treated. Related to fairness is necessary disciplining those for inappropriate behavior. It is critical that the discipline is meted fairly to prevent the culture of favoritism.
2. Accountability for errors demonstrates that the leader is strong and understanding and possesses character that will be respected by all. As humans we will make mistakes. As the founder of General Motors, Will Durant, stated: "Forget mistakes. Forget everything except what you're going to do now and do it. Today is your lucky day" [3].
3. The basis of excellent relationships, both personal and professional, is trustworthiness. Trust can be best defined as a unique behavior set, as acting in a manner that is dependent on another person; the belief that a person will act in a particular manner for a given situation, a mental frame of reference that someone is dependable or that he will do what he said, and a feeling with confidence and security that another individual or partner actually is concerned [4].
4. Honesty, which is closely related to trust, is the ability to discuss issues that are determined to be important and closely related to trust and is the ability to discuss any issues that are deemed to be important". Abraham Lincoln so aptly stated, "Resolve to be honest at all events; and if, in your own judgment, you cannot be an honest lawyer, resolve to be honest without being a lawyer. Choose some other occupation".

   Honesty in conjunction with the use of critical thinking to seek the truth must be the goal of everyone. Honesty provides confidence in ourselves and others and presents a positive self-image [5]. A study conducted by the American Psychological Association concluded that a person who tells the truth when tempted to lie can experience a significant improvement in his/her person's mental health [6].
5. Respect for others is demonstrated by the tolerance of differences, the use of good manners, being courteous and considerate, and the use of peaceful negotiations to resolve issues. This method to demonstrate respect can simply be stated as the treatment of others as you would have them treat you.
6. Responsibility is demonstrated by one who:
   a. Is consistent and dependable

b. Does what he says
c. Uses critical thinking before initiating action
d. Recognizes that all decisions have consequences
e. Takes responsibility for his decisions

Ethical leadership is critical to the development of a positive attitude in the workplace that results in productive relationships with individuals, teams, and the overall organization. Leaders who lead by example will cause other leaders to follow their example. This results in the assurance that employees, vendors, regulatory agencies, customers, and everyone with whom the organization interacts are treated equally and ethically. This includes the proper maintenance of equipment and the provision of a safe working environment for all employees [7].

2.2 What Are Some Examples of Decisions Made by Ethical Leadership?

2.2.1 *Installation of an individual incentive system in the sewing department of a furniture plant*

The author was a team member whose purpose was to install an incentive system in the sewing department of a furniture manufacturer that produced dinette tables and chairs. At one time the studies that were used to establish the incentive system may have existed but due to employee turnover and the history of financial instability of the company, that documentation was no longer available. Not all chair backs needed to be upholstered since some could be wooden inserts but all seats required an upholstery operation. The system was to replace an existing one for which little documentation existed. The covers to be sewn were fabric and vinyl of varying sizes and shapes that were upholstered over foam onto a particle board seat panel.

The author has installed several incentive systems as well as managing an existing one and making revisions as manufacturing process or material occurred in a unionized manufacturing plant. No grievance or complaint was ever registered against the author for the production standards established that served as the basis of an individual or group incentive system. The reason was that the author ensured that the rates were fair first for the individual and second for the company. The rationale for this priority was that without productive quality-oriented employees who satisfied their internal or external customers, the company would not be profitable and would eventually fail.

The team advised the management that due to the lack of confidence in the accuracy of the existing system and the inability to answer questions about the existing system due to the lack of documentation, the team would ensure that the accuracy level of the production standards was at least 95% and that all affected by the system would have confidence in results.

Prior to the initiation of the studies, the team met with the department supervisor and all the operators to explain the reason for the need of the new system, that a sufficient amount of all operators should understand the methodology and ask questions if clarification was needed, that the ambiguities that existed in the existing system would be eliminated, and that the new system would provide timely information as to their progress due to the use of barcodes author.

Before initiating studies the team asked itself the following question: if I were an operator, what steps should be taken to increase my confidence level in the new system given the problems with the old one? The primary problem with the old system was the inability to differentiate among covers based on the style of the chair and whether it was a seat or back. Seat covers were classified as small, medium, and large. Documentation did not exist to determine which chair models were small, medium, or large. Backs to be sewn were simply identified a back – thus all backs regardless of size or fabric type were assigned the same rate. A primary difference between a seat and back was that some seats were sewn with a border and welt cord and some backs were sewn together with foam which required a thicker thread line (see Figure 2.1) [8].

For covers that required to meet a different fire code standard, a different thread made of Kevlar was required.

The team agreed at a minimum the following was required and with the support of management would be provided:

A. Operators would be advised prior to the initiation of the studies concerning the start date and introduced to the practitioners who would be taking the studies.
B. Each cover to be sewn was to be assigned a unique part number.
C. Studies were to be taken to determine if there was a difference in sewing time for different styles of fabric versus vinyl, the type of thread used, and if there was a difference between sewing a straight seam versus a curved seam, the type of stitches, and stitch length.
D. Studies were to be taken to determine if there was a difference in handling time – gathering and preparing the needed components for the sewing process.

Figure 2.1   A sewn seat with welt cord and a border [8].

E. Each new cover would be assigned a unique part number to:
   1. Enable the construction of an accurate bill of material for costing and the use of Material Planning (MRP)
   2. Enable the development of standard data sheets to ensure the consistency of sewing time as a linear function of two variables, the distance sewn and the number of different components the operator needed to assemble prior to initiating the sewing process
   3. To increase the confidence level of the operators in the accuracy of the new system
   4. To enable the use of bar code technology to track orders in real time through the system and the calculation of incentive earnings

Formal time studies enabled the development of standard sewing times to meet standards to meet non-fire, fire codes and to satisfy the Leadership in Energy and Environmental Design (LEED) concerns.

The first action is taken to define precisely a unit that would satisfy the current situation and be applicable to all future sewn covers. Time studies revealed there was no statistical difference in the time needed to sew the different materials, fabric and vinyl, the addition of a border, or the inclusion of a welt cord using a folder. Due to potential changes in the material sewn and the methodology of the sewing process, the definition of unit sewn was expanded to include the chair style, the type of fabric used, the addition of a border, and the existence of a welt cord. Analysis of the data from the time studies revealed that the actual sewing time did not vary between sewing vinyl or varying thicknesses of fabric. Further study indicated that sewing an additional cut pattern of material to meet the increased needs of Environmental concerns as Leadership in Energy and Environmental Design (LEED) did had no effect on the sewing time [9].

To satisfy the current situation and potential changes, it was determined that a different part number would be created for each chair style, each type of material, and the existence of a border and welt cord.

Currently, the labor standard for sewing a chair style was the same regardless of the material used and the existence of a border and welt cord. To prevent future confusion and allow for expansion for the sewing of additional types of material and additional processes, a unique part number was assigned to each different cover sewn.

2.2.2 Management response to a misquoted sales price due to a computational error

As an example, a salesman quoted a price to a customer that was incorrect because the salesman did not consider the additional processes that would be required to produce the item to meet the customers needs. The President called the customer and guaranteed the quoted price for a year although a cost analysis of that item indicated that sales of that item to the customer would be at best a break even situation. The motivation behind that decision was that the salesman had shaken the hand of the Purchasing Agent (PA) and had looked him in the eye as the salesman provided the quote. The president did indicate that the price was subject to change after the year, but as a result of the failure of the salesman to follow protocol, the price that was quoted would be held for one year regardless of the volume sold. This company was led by someone who told me that the most important things are honesty, integrity, and reputation. He elaborated further and stated that you can always get more money but without those three things, money is meaningless.

2.2.3 The action of management after a misquoted price due to the failure of the salesman to ask relevant questions

The incorrect quote resulted from the failure of the salesman to read and fully comprehend the specifications provided to him by the PA. The salesman was aware that the company sold a competitor a similar product in a distant facility for what the salesman assumed to be a similar process and provided a quote based on that erroneous assumption. To meet the minimum requirements, the final product would require additional processes that were available at a distant plant. The quote did not include the costs of those additional processes or the freight costs from the plant to the customer.

As a result of this error, the president requested the help of the engineer to help design a flow chart to simplify the quoting process. This flow chart was presented at the next quarterly sales meeting for feedback and modified as a result of feedback.

2.2.4 *The acknowledgement of a vendor that failed to deliver material handling equipment to specification*

The author ordered a material handling system from a distant vendor that was to meet certain criteria. A critical specification was the ability to change from one size product to another within one minute. The author visited the vendor in the vendor's facility to witness a demonstration using various products manufactured at the author's plant that had been specifically produced, packaged, and shipped to the vendor. The demonstration required a changeover from one product to another. The author observed and recorded the time needed to complete the change. The time recorded was significantly greater than the time that was specified.

The vendor then realized that the equipment had not been modified as needed to ensure that changeovers could be completed within the specified time. The vendor then attempted to modify the equipment but soon realized that it was not possible. The vendor had spent many dollars in an effort to supply the equipment specified, but upon realizing that it was not possible, the vendor apologized to the author's time and money spent without the desired results.

2.2.5 *The purchase of livestock and reimbursement of farmers due to the improper installation of a change in a manufacturing process*

The author worked for a company that produced a paper product from recycled paper board. The company experimented with an additive to the adhesive to increase the strength of a paper product. One pound of the additive would result in sufficient gains in strength to offset the loss in strength due to reducing the amount of recycled paper board by one pound. The weight of the additive had to equal the weight of the loss of paperboard due to the requirement that the tare weights of the final product could not change. The costs of the additive were approximately one-tenth the costs of paperboard resulting in net savings. Manufacturing with the additive did not result in increased waste or a reduction in productivity.

This problem that followed the use of the additive was not anticipated, because at another plant that made the same change, the change was without incident. An investigation into the reasons for problems at the second installation revealed that the first plant was connected to the city water sewage system whereas the second plant used a septic tank for the disposal of wastewater and sewage. Some of the additives had leaked into groundwater that fed a stream that was used for drinking water for livestock.

This costly mistake could have been avoided if the decision-maker had asked one critical question – what is the difference between processes between the two plants? The failure to ask this one question resulted in fines, penalties, and a tarnished reputation.

2.2.6 *The shifting of production to take advantage of lower off-peak rates*

The initial motivation for the change was financial but the decision was also an ethical one. The decision to shift production to off-peak hours enabled the utility company to supply energy to meet the demand of other companies to prevent rolling blackouts and the need to add capacity by the construction of coal-fired facilities.

This example is fully discussed in Chapter 4.

2.2.7 *The establishment of a safety team*

The members of the team represented each department of the plant. The meetings began in the conference room where any concerns or questions were addressed. The team then toured each department of the plant making observations on each operator. The team then reconvened to the conference room to share good safety practices observed as well as those that needed improvement. Both practices were noted in the minutes which were distributed to other plants within the company.

As a result, other plants adopted the good practices and made recommendations for improvement. The author, as team leader, purchased a red polo-type shirt for each member of the safety team, and they wore it on the day of scheduled safety team meetings. The shirt was embroidered with the company logo and the term "Safety team member" in a contrasting color. The team was further rewarded at company expense by attending a company picnic at a distant location for further recognition by upper management.

The increased engagement of all employees and the support of all levels of management resulted in significant reductions in accident and incident rates.

2.3 What Are the Requirements for Ethical Decisions?

2.3.1 The ethical decision-maker must consider all the ramifications of the decision

1. The ethical decision-maker must consider all the ramifications of the decision on all those entities affected by the decision similar to the physician who adheres to the Oath of Hippocrates that prioritizes the responsibilities of members to patients first, society, other health professionals, and then to himself [10].

The ethical decision-maker must recognize that decision-making is not a zero-sum game but one that requires compromise. The goal of an ethical decision is to maximize the value of the decision to all those affected by the decision.

2.3.2 The ethical decision-maker must prioritize the benefits and costs of all decisions

2. The ethical decision-maker must prioritize the benefits and costs of all decisions to those affected, which include fellow decision-makers, employees, customers, vendors, regulatory agencies, and the environment [11].

The decision-maker must acknowledge that the results of previous decisions have caused irreparable damage to the world's population and to the environment [12]. A few of these would include the use of asbestos in insulation which can cause non-cancerous abnormalities and other diseases [13], and the use of lead in paint, gasoline, and pipes which was declared to be a public health hazard because it can cause learning and other disabilities [14], and deforestation that results in soil erosion, an increase in flooding, and the release of carbon dioxide and other greenhouse gases [15].

As a result, the decision-maker, now more than ever, must investigate all consequences of a decision to ensure that both the long- and short-term benefits outweigh the costs. Metrics for benefits and costs include dollars, quality of life, and mean life span.

2.4 What Are Some Examples of Decisions Made by Unethical Leaders?

2.4.1 *The unethical installation of an incentive system*

An example involving the installation of incentive rates of an unethical but legal situation occurred in a plant that manufactured various window coverings as horizontal mini-blinds for windows and vertical blinds for sliding glass doors. Some of the processes were automated but a majority were labor-intensive. The facility operated two shifts six days a week and employed more than 400 employees. Annual sales of this company exceeded $100 million dollars.

The new president hired an outside consulting firm to install various individual incentive systems for all production employees to reduce direct labor costs. The consulting firm was to complete the assignment within two weeks. Due to numerous complaints from employees that the rates were incorrect, the author was hired as an outside consultant to evaluate the newly installed rates and to make recommendations.

The author examined the rates and reported that the rates were reasonable and fair to both the employees and the company based on time studies taken by the author. The author also reported that in his opinion the complaints were legitimate and were due to numerous failures on the part of the company. The first failure was there was no documentation as to how the rates were established. At a minimum, the documentation should include individual time studies with elemental descriptions. Time studies would include the date taken, the operator, the operation, the person taking the time study, the times for each repetition, the mean and standard deviation for repetition, the times for each task, the mean and standard deviation for each task, the necessary calculations to obtain the mean time for each task, the percentage allowed for fatigue, personal time and delay, and the assigned rating factor.

There was also no documentation indicating the management and employees were advised in advance concerning the appearance of the consulting company or the purpose of their visit, participation of management and the plant engineer in the studies, an explanation to employees of derivation or the actual value of the standards, their computation or the effect that implementation of the standards would have on their compensation, and more importantly, the necessary training for employees to enable them to meet or exceed their standards.

After implementation employees were advised that any employee who did not meet or exceed his production standard would be fired. The author was shocked that such a drastic action would be taken in a short period of time due to the lack of information provided to the employees, particularly the training that may be needed to ensure that employees attain or exceed the goals.

The author learned that one employee who had over 19 years of experience in her current position was about to lose her job due to not meeting her production requirements. I asked management if I could work with her to determine what changes she should make in order to meet the requirements to avoid termination. Management agreed and within four hours she was not only meeting requirements but exceeding them. The author checked her production for the next several days to ensure that she maintained that same level of production. The author also worked with several other operators who were about to be terminated due to failure to meet their production goals. All of the operators were able to avoid termination by meeting the production goals.

The author also worked with the plant engineer to ensure that the plant engineer would be able to train other employees to attain standards after the author's contract expired.

This experience in the establishment and implementation of individual incentive rates was unethical for the many reasons stated above. As a result, many of the employees complained to authorities and within several years the plant closed, resulting in the loss of over 400 jobs.

2.4.2 The unethical and illegal attempt to install an incentive sales program

An example of an unethical and illegal attempt to install an incentive sales program system occurred after the merger of Wells Fargo Bank, based in CA, and Northwest, based in MN, in 1998. Prior to the merger, the two banks were rated 10th and 11th in the country in the banking industry [16].

The stated reason for the merger, according to the chairman of Northwest, Richard Kovacevich, was to expose new customers to numerous services and in particular the opportunities and benefits of cross-selling. Mr. Kovacevich became the president and CEO of the recently merged organization, which retained the Wells Fargo name [16].

Cross-selling refers to the offering of potential sales for additional products or services based on the interest of the customer or the actual purchase of an existing product. The practice can result in an increase in customer loyalty, value, and retention. Another practice designed to increase sales is upselling through the purchase of an existing product. An example of cross-selling in the hotel/motel industry can occur when a newlywed couple checks into a hotel/motel and is offered the opportunity to purchase champagne, flowers, or chocolate. An example in the same industry of upselling would occur if the couple is offered a room with a better view for an upcharge. Both are intended to increase revenue [17].

Although the Wells Fargo that existed prior to the merger had an internal "Sales Quality Manual" that mandated the prior agreement of all customers to all products and services that were sold to them, after the merger pressure to engage in cross-selling was intense. The new Wells Fargo developed a sales incentive program that not only rewarded cross-selling extremely well but also penalized those employees whose performance was substandard. As a result of the unrealistic sales goals given to employees, many fell victim to the pressure to attain these goals and voluntarily left their employment. Many of those employees who were unable to meet their sales targets were told that they were subject to termination.

The result of this sales incentive program was the generation of additional revenue in the amount of 2.6 million dollars due to the creation of 115,000 unauthorized accounts and credit cards. As a result of an investigation by the *LA Times* in 2013, the LA city attorney, and the US comptroller of the currency, Wells Fargo was found guilty of fraud and agreed to a fine of $185 million and an additional $5 million for customer remediation. Although the senior vice president for community banking who managed over 6,000 branches resigned in 2016 in which over two million customers had deposit and credit card accounts opened against their knowledge, she retained her position despite the fact that these employees who were her responsibility committed fraud. Over 5,000 (5,300) of these employees who averaged earning between $11.75 and $16.50 per hour were laid off. During the three-year period from over the period 2009 to 2016, this senior vice president earned 27 million in compensation. Upon her retirement in December 2016, she anticipates a total of 125 million in bank equity and stock options. On her announcement of her impending resignation, the CEO, Mr. John Stumph, stated that she was a valued and trusted employee and a "role model for responsible, principled and inclusive leadership" [18].

References

1. Difference between right and wrong. (n.d.) Retrieved 8/1/2022 from: https://www.bing.com/search?q=difference%20between%20right%20and%20wrong&form=SWAUA2
2. Importance and requirements for ethical leadership in an organization. (n.d.). Norwhich University. Retrieved 3/14/2022 from: https://online.norwich.edu/academic-programs/resources/importance-of-ethical-leadership
3. "Today is your lucky day." – Will Durant Founder of GM, 23 Jan 2019[25]. *Good News Network Quote of the Day*. Retrieved 4/22/2022 from: https://www.goodnewsnetwork.org/will-durant-quote-your-lucky-day/
4. Thagard, P., PhD. (2018). What is trust? *Psychology Today*. Retrieved 3/22/2022 from: https://www.psychologytoday.com/us/blog/h ot-thought/201810/what-is-trust
5. Conners, C.D. Honesty- how it benefits you and others. *Mission.Org*. Retrieved 6/11/2022 from: https://medium.com/the-mission/honesty-how-it-benefits-you-and-others-ecb3e7fabb9a
6. Kelly, A. (2012). A life without lies: How living honestly can affect health. Session 3189, 12 to 12:50 p.m., Saturday, Aug. 4, Room W303C, Level III, Orange County Convention Center. Retrieved 5/11/2022 from https://www.apa.org/news/press/releases/2012/08/lying-less
7. What is ethical leadership. (2022). Conduct led by values, vision, voice and virtue. Retrieved 7/22/2022 from: https://www.villanovau.com/resources/leadership/what-is-ethical-leadership/
8. Images of a sewn seat with weltcord and a border [30]. Retrieved 6/23/2022 from: https://www.bing.com/search?q=picture%20of%20a%20sewn%20seat%20with%20weltcord%20and%20border&form=SWAUA2
9. Leed. (n.d.). Retrieved 5/22/2022 from: https://www.bing.com/images/search?q=leed&cbn=KnowledgeCard&stid=b50fff77-46e2-08fc-210b-47f7b0676eb2&form=KCHIMM&first=1&tsc=ImageHoverTitle
10. Hajor, R. (2017). The physician's oath: Historical perspectives. *Heart Views*. Oct-Dec;18(4), 154–159. Retrieved 10/23/2022 from: https://www.ncbi.nlm.nih.gov/pmc/articles/PMC5755201/#:~:text=It%20is%20generally%20believed%20that%20the%20famous%20phrase%2C,or%20to%20do%20no%20harm%20.%E2%80%9D%20%5B%208%5D

11. Bonde, S, and Firenze, P. (2013). Awareness in international collaboration: A contextual approach. *Program in Science and Technology*. Brown University. Retrieved 7/30/2022 from: https://www.brown.edu/academics/science-and -technology-studies/framework-making-ethical-decisions
12. Ahmed, A. (2019). Definition of stewardship. Retrieved 6/12/2022 from: https:// bizfluent.com/about-4612393-definition-of-stewardship.html
13. The Agency for Toxic Substances and Disease Registry. (n.d.). Retrieved 2/22/2022 from: https://www.cdc.gov/nceh/lead/prevention/sources/paint.htm
14. The Agency for Toxic Substances and Disease Registry. (n.d.). Retrieved 2/22/2022 from: https://www.atsdr.cdc.gov/asbestos/health_effects_asbestos .htmln
15. Effects of Deforestation. (n.d.). Retrieved 3/25/2022 from: https://www.bing .com/search?q=effects+of+deforestation&qs=AS&pq=effects+of+def&sc=10-14 &cvid=7022ED0555DF42B09EDB03001F163232&FORM=QBRE&sp=1
16. Chang, V., O'Reilly, C., and Pfeffer, J. (2004). Wells Fargo and Northwest, "Merger of Equals". *Stanford Business*. Retrieved 6/15/2022 from: https://www .gsb.stanford.edu/faculty-research/case-studies/wells-fargo-norwest-merger -equals-b
17. Gibson, A, (2021). Cross-selling versus upselling: What is more optimal in the hotel industry. Retreived 6/15/2022 from: https://www.upstay.tech/cross-selling -vs-upselling-what-is-more-optimal-in-the-hotel-industry/
18. Sridharan, U.V. @ Hadley; L.U. (2018). Internal audit, fraud and risk management. *International Journal of the Academic Business World*. Spring 2018. Retrieved 16 June 2022 from: https://jwpress.com/Journals/IJABW/BackIssues /IJABW-Spring-2018

Chapter 3

Productivity, Efficiency, and Machine Downtime

3.1 Brief Explanation of Productivity, Efficiency, and Machine Downtime

Productivity, expressed as a percent, is the ratio of output and input for a specific time period, as an eight-hour shift, a week or a month, The term can apply to a work center, an assembly line, a specific machine or group of machines or an entire facility. It is usually refers to a manufacturing operation but could be adapted to any activity that has outputs and uses inputs to achieve the outputs. As an example, productivity of an automobile service center whose only service to change motor oil and filter I would be ratio of automobiles serviced to the number of automobiles that could be serviced in a specific time period, as an eight hour day. Another example would be a health clinic whose only purpose is to administer vaccines. Productivity for the clinic would be the ratio of the number of vaccines given during a certain period to the number that could be administered during that same time period. In these and all other situations, a calculated productivity of less than 100 percent represents opportunities to provide additional services.

Output can be materials, products, goods, or services, whereas input includes employees, equipment, material, units of energy, relevant information, land, and financial resources [1].

Efficiency, expressed as a percent, is the ratio of output to input during the period that the operation, process, or an assembly line is actually in operation.

DOI: 10.4324/9781003302308-3

Machine downtime, expressed as a percent, is the ratio of the time that a machine, assembly line, or entire plant does not operate to the time that the process, assembly line, or entire plant was scheduled to operate. There are a myriad of reasons for downtime, such as a lack of the correct material, a mechanical malfunction, an electrical outage, etc.

All three are examples of key performance indicators (KPIs) that can be used to measure progress toward a goal. A KPI is a quantifiable measurement used by an organization to indicate progress toward a certain goal. Its emphasis is improvement, both strategic and operational. Other KPIs include revenue growth, gross profit margin, accident and incident ratios, and cost of quality [2].

3.2 Definitions of Productivity, Efficiency, and Machine Downtime

1. Productivity is a ratio, usually expressed as a percent, that measures the relationship between total outputs and total inputs, or simply how well resources are managed during the time frame that the operation, assembly line, or entire plant is scheduled to function. The time frame may be an hour, shift, week, etc.

The concept of 'productivity', a measure of the usage of resources, can be applied to all resources, but the term 'productivity' usually refers to those resources that include direct and/or indirect labor. 'Utilization' is a term that is used to measure how well other resources are used. For example, material utilization is ratio, expressed as a percent of 100. of the material that remains after processing to the amount of material that began the process, As an example, if components of chair are cut from a 10 ft x 5 ft sheet of plywood that consumes 40 of the 50 square feet available, then the material utilization would be the ratio of usable output, or 40 sq ft, to amount of material that entered the process, or 50 sq ft. The material utilization in this example would be 80 percent. Another measure for material utilization is waste percent. In this situation the process began with 100 percent and utilized 80 percent of the material which yields a waste percent of 20 percent. Waste reduction can contribute significantly to an improvement in profitability. The percent of material utilization and waste for each material will sum to 100 percent. The utilization of a container used to ship material is the ratio of the material in the container to be shipped to the maximum amount of material that the container can hold. The units of measurements for both must be identical. These units can be pounds, gallons, bushels, etc. Each percentage will vary from 0% – an empty container – to 100% – a container fully loaded. Shipping costs will vary inversely with utilization.

In manufacturing the most common application is direct labor productivity defined as the ratio of the amount of work in a time period done by a specified crew size with a required level of training compared to the amount of work that should have been done during that time period by the specified crew employing standardized procedures. Output is measured in man-hours earned: input is the number of actual hours used to earn the calculated man-hours. The value will range from 0 to 100, with 0 meaning poor utilization and 100 representing a maximum output with the existing materials, equipment, working conditions, and the skill level of employees.

The term can also be used to measure indirect labor. Based on the experience of the author, this measurement is seldom taken for several reasons. The first is that due to the variety of tasks performed by employees who perform such tasks and the location of the work to be performed, determining the amount of work to be performed would be an impossible task. The tasks often require moving from one area to another, performing tasks that vary from unloading shipments to moving components to needed areas. Another reason is that the number of employees usually involved in indirect labor is small compared to the number in direct labor, meaning that the costs of obtaining that value would greatly exceed the potential benefits.

Indirect labor should be measured using a technique such as work sampling,

The goal for its measurement differs from that of measuring direct labor. The goal of direct labor productivity is 100%, whereas the goal for indirect labor is a percentage greater than 0% but less than 100%. An indirect labor percent that is too low represents an underutilized resource and results in excessive labor cost. A 100% indirect labor could possibly cause delays in the unloading of material, providing needed supplies for production, etc. The cost of these delays, if able to be calculated, would probably exceed the costs for the unforced idle time that any under-utilized indirect labor employees would incur. The percentage will vary with the situation and should be monitored and adjusted as needed employing work sampling. Indirect labor, including its calculation and use, is fully explained below.

The term 'productivity' can also be applied to the utilization of materials. As in labor productivity, material utilization is the ratio of raw material output to the raw material used to produce the output. The units used to calculate this ratio must be the same and can be pounds, tons, square feet, each, etc. As in labor productivity, the material utilization will vary from 0 to

1; the greater the material utilization, the better the use of the resource. In lieu of material productivity, the author employed the term 'waste percentage', which had a greater comprehension.

'Waste percentage' is not the percentage of material used in production but instead the percentage of material lost during the various processes of manufacturing. The term 'waste' is easier to associate with lost opportunities and potential income. The waste percentage for each process should be determined and studies conducted for potential reduction. A reduction of waste represents potential income, which would vary directly with the percentage. Often a small reduction in waste can result in huge savings.

As an example to demonstrate potential savings that can result from reducing material waste, the author worked for a paper converting company that produced a paper tube that was crimped on one end to accommodate a cap inserted into the crimp to hold the tube in place while yarn or filament was wound onto the tube. The tube was produced ¾ inches longer to accommodate the cap used by this customer. The author calculated potential savings that would result from reducing the extra length from ¾ to ½ inch per tube.

Prior to making the change, the vendor was made aware of the potential requested change in the size of the cap and the reason for the change. Due to the excellent working relationship between the customer and the vendor,

Figure 3.1 Paper tubes with one end turned in or crimped [3].

the customer was very receptive since as the customer stated, these realized savings would postpone future price increases for the tubes. The new caps were ordered and upon receipt, the changes in the tubes were made. The net savings exceeded $80,000. Replacing the caps was the ethical and proper action since the beneficiary was the company making the tubes.

Several crimped paper tubes can be seen below. Plastic caps would be inserted into both ends; only the cap that was inserted into the crimped end changed.

The term 'productivity' can also be applied to the consumption of various types of energy. Energy productivity is the ratio of output to the amount of energy used to produce that level of output.

Energy productivity measures the economic benefit from each unit of energy consumed to produce that level of economic benefit. On a national scale, it is the ratio of total economic output, as GDP to the amount of energy consumed as barrels of oil equivalent or kilowatt hours of electricity [4].

The author has not used this productivity calculation due to the complexity of computing energy usage used when several different types are employed and output due to a variety of products produced which use varying quantities of different types of energy. The author has successfully reduced the costs of energy by focusing on one type in a certain application.

The initial motivation for the change was financial, but the decision was also an ethical one. The decision to shift production to off-peak hours enabled the utility company to supply energy to meet the demand of other companies to prevent rolling blackouts and the need to add capacity by the construction of coal-fired facilities.

For example, he worked with an engineer at a company recycling paper board. The first step in the analysis was to select the process which consumed the most energy. The second was to determine if the energy costs of that process, which was drying the paper board after it was formed, could be isolated from the total costs of the energy. The drying process used steam produced in a boiler that used natural gas and was transmitted to a number of drums that were driven by 50-horsepower electric motors. The use of natural gas was confined to the boiler, and the electric bill was decomposed to show usage by the motor by each hour of usage. Thus, the calculation of energy costs by process was possible.

Paperboard has various grades, densities, and calipers to meet certain specifications. This paper mill produced the highest grade of paperboard during the first shift due to the greater supervision and availability of laboratory personnel. The utilities providing electricity and natural gas charged a different rate depending on the time used. After determining the total, natural gas and electricity, costs of drying per ton of board produced on the first shift, the company calculated the costs for producing during off-peak hours – the third shift – and realized that the savings realized would be more than sufficient to pay for additional supervision and laboratory personal to work on the third shift.

A similar reduction in utility costs was realized by a company that manufactured fiberglass insulation as a result of shifting the drying process from on-peak to off-peak hours. The primary motivation for these changes was cost reductions which are essential to the long-term success of any organization. Benefits of cost reductions are quantifiable and easy to comprehend. Other long-term benefits as potential reduction in greenhouse emissions exist but are not as quantifiable and meaningful as cost reductions. An expanded definition of ethics, as based on philosophers as Jeremy Bentham, is making decisions that create the most value for society. If this is used as a definition of ethical behavior, then these decisions would be classified as ethical [5].

Productivity exceeding 100% is an indication of one of the following:

1. An error made during calculation.
2. A reporting error in the number of products produced or in the number of man-hours consumed during the production of the reported quantity.
3. There has been a change in materials, equipment, or the skill level of employees since the initial establishment of the standards.
4. The existing standards are incorrect.

Recommended prevention strategies for each situation:

1. Double-check calculations, compare results with previous calculations to ensure consistency.
2. Ensure that employees involved in the reporting of data understand the criticality of accurate information. Intentional misrepresentation of data is unethical and can result in incorrect decisions.
3. A continuation of this situation should initiate a thorough review of the existing standards for potential revision. Prior to the initiation of new studies, complete a review of the documentation used to establish the existing standards to enable a comparison with existing conditions, including equipment, materials, and employees. This comparison may reveal the use of a different material, the use of a new or different fixture, a new or different process, a modified work station, or a change in the skill level needed. The ability to make this comparison accurately is the reason that

accurate elemental descriptions must be documented and maintained. See glossary for definition and examples of elemental descriptions.

4. Efficiency expressed as a percent is similar to productivity since both are a measure of resource utilization expressed as a ratio during the period the machine or process is in operation The conditions required to compute productivity are also needed to compute efficiency. Similar to productivity, values for efficiency can vary between 0 and 100.

The efficiency percentage will equal or exceed the productivity percentage. The productivity percentage plus the downtime percentage should equal 100% because during the period the machine is scheduled to operate, the machine is either producing or not.

5. Machine idle time expressed as a percent is the time that a process, an assembly line, or an entire plant does not produce quality products. The various reasons should be documented in detail to enable appropriate plans to decrease machine idle time. These plans could involve the development of new products, marketing strategies, training classes for employees, or preventive maintenance programs. The ultimate goal should be to achieve zero machine idle time.

3.3 The Meaning of X Percent Productivity, Efficiency, and Machine Downtime

1. A calculated productivity represents the percent of work that was completed compared to the amount of work that should have been accomplished during the time that a process or machine is scheduled to operate for a specific interval of time, as in an hour, day, etc. This percentage can vary from 0 to 100. The amount of work that should have been done must be established by industrial engineering professionals to ensure credibility. A calculated productivity for a period of less than 100% represents the percent of productivity lost during the period.

2. Efficiency represents the amount of work completed during the time the machine or process is functional compared to the actual amount of work that was actually completed during that same period for a specific interval of time, as in an hour, day, etc. This percentage can vary from 0 to 100.

3. Machine downtime represents the percentage of time that a process or machine is unable to operate to produce quality products due to a lack of orders, a lack of material, or direct labor or unscheduled

maintenance. Unlike productivity and efficiency, a high number is not desirable since it represents lost productivity.

3.4 The Computation and Interpretation of Productivity, Efficiency, and Machine Downtime

Productivity is the ratio of the amount of work that was completed to the amount of work that should have been accomplished during a certain period of time. The amount of work accomplished is measured in standard labor man-hours and divided by the actual number of man-hours consumed to earn those standard hours to calculate productivity. Each item manufactured will earn a specified number of standard hours based on the number of processes required, the complexity of those processes, and the standard crew size.

In order to better understand the relationship among productivity, machine efficiency, and machine downtime, consider the following situation. The industrial engineering department has established a production standard on machine A of ten units per machine hour with a trained crew of three. The standard man-hours per unit were 30, 10 units per machine hour or 0.10 machine hours per unit multiplied by the standard crew size of 3 per machine hour which yields the standard of 0.30 man-hours per unit. The machine was scheduled to begin production at 7 am, the normal start time for the first shift. For one of a myriad of reasons, the machine did not begin production until 9 am; thus there was a 2-hour delay before the machine was not able to produce quality products. The cause of the delay could be a lack of the correct material, an electrical pneumatic, or mechanical problem, etc.

The crew began producing quality products at 9 am and was able to continue until the end of the 8-hour shift. During the 6 hours the machine operated, 60 quality products were manufactured. The number of man-hours earned is the product of the number of units produced (60) and the standard man-hours per item (0.30), or 18. The number of man-hours scheduled is the product of the number of machine hours scheduled (8) and the standard crew size of three per machine hour (3), or 24 man-hours.

Productivity is the ratio of standard man-hours earned and the number of man-hours scheduled. A productivity of 100% would represent the maximum production of a machine given its current mechanical status and the skill level of the assigned crew. A calculated productivity level exceeding 100% should initiate studies to investigate potential changes for standard revision. In the above situation, the productivity calculation would be the ratio of the standard man-hours earned (18) and the number of man-hours the machine was scheduled (the product of 8 hours and the standard crew of 3 or 24), or 75%. A productivity of less than 100% represents lost production due to downtime which will negatively affect the direct labor costs, profit levels, and scheduling.

Efficiency is the ratio of standard man-hours earned while in operation to the ratio of man-hours the machine was in operation. For this situation efficiency is the ratio of the standard man-hours earned (18) and the standard man-hours of the machine during operation (6 times the standard crew size of 3 or 18), yielding an efficiency of 100%. An efficiency of 100 means that the crew met expectations. An efficiency exceeding 100 is an indication of either an incorrect standard or a reporting error either in the hours that a machine was in operation or in the crew size. Regardless of the reason, an investigation should be initiated to remedy the error.

Downtime, or the time expressed as a percent, is the ratio of the number of hours the machine was not producing quality products (2) to the number of hours that production was scheduled. In this situation, the percentage is (2 hours down/8 hours scheduled) 25%. As in efficiency, this represents lost production and the reasons for the downtime must be fully documented to enable the development of a plan to address the reasons for mitigation. Downtime is a costly expense. Potential solutions could be a preventive maintenance program or improved communications between the warehouse and production to ensure that the correct raw material is delivered as needed.

3.5 An Example to Demonstrate the Calculation of Productivity, Efficiency, and Machine Downtime

3.5.1 The calculation of productivity

The productivity of an upholsterer in a furniture plant would be the ratio of the number of chairs, ottomans, or sofas of a certain style produced in a specified time period to the number of chairs. Time studies will determine the standard hours required for each product as well as each additional feature the customer requests. One such feature is brass nail trim. If the customer orders this feature, then the standard hours required to attach the brass nails will be added to the standard hours needed to upholster the item. In addition, the cost of the brass nails based on the quantity used would be added to the costs. The purchased costs of brass nails used for trim is the quantity used as expressed in terms of the purchasing unit and the cost of the nails per purchasing unit. For example the quantity of brass

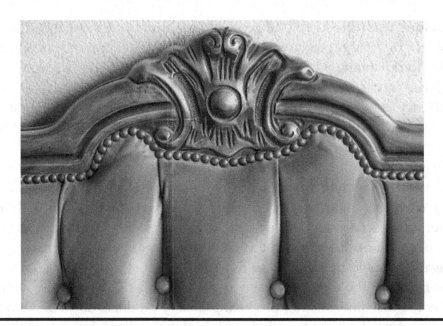

Figure 3.2 An upholstered chair with brass nail trim [6].

nails in the bill of materials (BOM) is expressed in terms of the purchase unit of measure. If the purchasing unit of measure is each, and 250 brass nails used, then the quantity in the BOM will be 250. If the purchase unit of measure is thousand (M), then the quantity of brass nails in the BOM would be 0.250. To confirm an accurate material cost roll up for the brass nail trim, if the cost of each brass nail is $0.12 and the purchase unit of measure is each, then the material cost of the brass nails would be $30.00, the quantity of 250 multiplied by the cost of each $0.12. If the purchasing unit of measure is thousands, M, then the cost roll up for the brass nail trim would be the cost of the brass nails ($12.00 per M) multiplied by the quantity in the BOM (0.250) that would yield a cost of $3.00 for the brass nails feature. The cost of the brass nails, as well as all other material costs, must include the freight costs to the manufacturing plant.

As can be seen in Table 3.1, the overall productivity of this upholsterer is 85%. Since there was no reported downtime, the efficiency would be 85%. Standard direct labor costs are based on a productivity of 100%. In this situation, the actual costs for these would exceed the standard costs, and the labor variance for the sofa would be higher than the other two items produced during that period due to lower productivity. In fact the direct labor costs for the sofa would be approximately double the standard costs. The direct labor variance is the reciprocal of productivity; for the sofa, the direct labor variance is (1/0.45) 122%.

Table 3.1   Calculation of Productivity

	Chair Stair 1	*Chair Style 2*	*Sofa Style 1*	*Total*
Standard hours per item	0.252	0.315	0.668	
Completed items	14	11	1	26
Standard hours earned	3.528	3.465	0.668	7.661
Actual hours used for production	4	3.5	1.5	9
Productivity each item	88%	99%	45%	85%

The industrial engineering continuous team needs to evaluate the standards for the sofa. The initial step would be to time study this upholsterer – with the permission of management and the employee and compare normal times for each task to discern the difference. If the total difference exceeds 10%, then a formal time study needs to be conducted on at least one other upholsterer to determine the causes of the discrepancy.

The discrepancies could exist for several reasons:

1. The particular upholsterer is not following the methods as specified in the time study.
2. This particular upholsterer needs additional training.
3. The standard for this sofa needs to be reevaluated.

This situation needs to be resolved as quickly as possible to prevent further losses in direct labor costs and to improve scheduling.

3.5.2 The calculation of efficiency

At the beginning of the shift, the upholsterer realizes that there is a leak in his air hose that feeds the staple gun used in the upholstery process. He immediately contacts his supervisor who notifies maintenance of the problem. Maintenance replaces the hose with a new one which requires 15 minutes or a total of 0.25 hours. As seen in Table 3.2, the downtime has no effect on overall productivity, but it reduces overall efficiency from 100% to 90%.

Efficiency measures the amount of work that was completed during the period that a process or machine was in operation to the amount of work that should have been accomplished during a certain period of time. Similar to the calculation of productivity, the two would differ if there was a period of time when the process or machine was not able to produce quality

Table 3.2 Calculation of Productivity and Efficiency

	Chair Style 1	*Chair Style 2*	*Sofa Style 1*	*Total*
Standard hours per item	0.252	0.315	0.668	
Completed items	14	11	1	26
Standard hours earned	3.528	3.465	0.668	7.661
Hours used for production	4.00	3.5	1.5	9
Productivity	88%	99%	45%	85%
Downtime to leak in air hose	0.25	0	0	0.25
Run time	3.75	3.5	1.5	8.75
Efficiency	94%	99%	45%	88%
Downtime percentage	6.25%	0.00%	0.00%	2.78%

products for any of the reasons previously discussed. This period of time, referred to as downtime, will reduce the time that the process or machine was able to function. Downtime must be recorded as well as the reasons for the downtime for analysis. Any amount of downtime will be subtracted from the amount of time the process or machine is scheduled to operate to yield actual run hours. Actual run hours will equal or be less than scheduled hours due to the unplanned downtime; consequently, the percentage for efficiency will be equal to or greater than productivity.

A change in the productivity of a given process can represent the effect of a change in a process, a material, the skill level of the assigned crew, or a different crew size. The degree of change and the cause for the change must be investigated to ensure that the change is cost effective. For example, a change in the material used may affect the manufacturing process time or the percentage of waste or the number of defects produced. A change in the manufacturing process as a result of a workplace redesign or use of a different fixture may affect process time, crew size or needed training, or the percentage of quality products or services produced. The goal of continual improvement requires accurate and complete documentation.

3.5.3 The calculation of downtime

Downtime percentage is the ratio of the total time that a machine, process, assembly line, or plant is unable to produce quality products due to a machine malfunction, the lack of needed components, the lack of a skilled crew, etc.

The downtime must be recorded as well as the reason for the downtime for analysis to determine reasons for the downtime to develop a maintenance plan to reduce unscheduled downtime.

Downtime begins when the process no longer produces quality parts and ends as the process begins to produce quality parts.

3.6 Methods to Measure Work

There are several techniques that can be used by a professional to measure the amount of work that should be performed in a certain period of time by a skilled employee using a specified procedure using designated tooling and fixtures under specific working conditions. A manufacturing facility is one that provides those conditions that can be controlled to enable the accurate measurement of work.

The common unit for measured work is the standard man-hour. A standard man-hour is the hours earned by an average employee working at a normal pace assigned to a certain task that includes allowances for fatigue, delay, and personal time added. The percentage for allowances will vary from work environment to environment.

Productivity is the ratio of standard hours earned to the actual assigned number of man-hours used to earn the standard hours. Actual man-hours used can be retrieved from the time clock or employee. The number of standard hours earned for each process requires a detailed study by an experienced practitioner. Prior to the initiation to develop standard man-hours for a process, the process must be evaluated for potential improvements. Conducting studies to determine the standard man-hours for a process without making potential improvements is a waste of resources and may result in an inflated value [7].

These techniques include (1) a formal time study, (2) work sampling, (3) group timing techniques, (4) predetermined time systems, and (5) estimates including input from employees. Each has its own advantages and disadvantages.

3.6.1 The formal time study which is the preferred method of the author

1. The author prefers the formal time study for a variety of reasons. This method, appropriate for a repetitive operation performed under normal

working conditions, enables the time study person to interact with the operator to evaluate the current method to seek potential improvement opportunities. Based on the experience of the author, the current method is used for two main reasons:

A. It has always been done this way.
B. No one ever asked if the process needed to be performed at all or how it can be improved.

Improvement may result from the use of a fixture, a redesign of the work station (see ergonomics in the glossary), or a reassignment of some tasks from one operator to another. Prior to the reassignment, cross-training must occur.

Before beginning the first study, after notifying management and the union if one exists, the first step is to introduce yourself to the person or persons who will perform the task to explain the purpose and the uses of the studies. During the introduction, the person conducting the study will explain the techniques that will be used to conduct the study, that questions can be asked at any time, and that the results will be discussed in detail with all the operators who participated in the study.

If the process to be studied is one on an assembly line, the practitioner must first identify the bottleneck operation. The improvement in the methods on an assembly line with multiple operators must begin with the identification of the bottleneck or the slowest operation on the line. Similar to the slowest car in a lane, no one can pass the car safely until there is sufficient room for the car to pass.

Identification of a bottleneck requires several random observations of the line to determine the workstation that has an accumulation of work to be done. If there is more than one bottleneck, the one performing the time study should select either one as a starting point.

Formal time studies can be used to develop a standard data sheet for a process that contains tasks that will not vary from iteration to iteration and tasks that will vary as a function of some constant.

The author used numerous time studies to develop a standard data sheet for the sewing operation of seat covers. The tasks whose performance times will be constant from iteration to iteration include obtaining the item to be sewn and placing it on the side border of the sewing table under the needle, attaching a pre-glued bar code sticker containing the part number, the date the item was sewn and the operator number, and placing the sewn cover onto the adjacent conveyor belt. The sewing time varied directly with the circumference of the cover and the material to be sewn. The mean times and standard deviation for those tasks with times were consistent among iterations and were calculated to ensure that the data was statistically significant.

This information was used to develop the standard data sheet for the sewing department. The header for the standard data sheet consisted of the date, the part number for the cover for which the standard sewing time was being calculated, the inches to be sewn, and the engineer performing the calculation. The rows on the standard data sheet contained all the tasks that needed to be performed, a column for the total of the mean times for each task, and a percentage for allowances.

3.6.2 *Work sampling which is frequently referred to as "Activity Sampling"*

2. Work sampling, which is frequently referred to as "Activity Sampling" or "Ratio Delay Study", is a statistical method first devised by L.H.S. Tippet in 1934.

   The use of work sampling has two objectives:

   A. To measure activities and delays while an operator is working or not working.

   B. To approximate the number of operators needed to perform an indirect labor operation, as loading and unloading material, resupplying a workstation, etc.

The theory, based on statistics, concludes that the percentage of observations recorded on an operation in any state is a reliable estimate of the percentage time the operation requires. The number of observations that need to be taken will vary inversely with the level of confidence desired from the study. The author used a confidence level of 90% [8].

While conducting the study to record an observation of working, the operator must be performing tasks that will add value to the product. No conclusions can be made from the percentage of not working except that the operator is not performing tasks that will add value to the product [9].

This method was employed by the author to determine the number of employees needed for indirect operations as warehousing. Before initiation studies, a table for making observations must be developed using a random number table. Times selected should not include scheduled break or lunch periods or times that are close to the scheduled breaks or at the beginning or end of the shift. The next task is to clearly define work and non-work activities. The observer notes at a random time if the person being studied is working or not working. Studies should be conducted over several days using different random times.

Results from work sampling studies should only be used as an indication of potential opportunities for improvement. As an example, consider the results of a work sampling study of employees in a warehouse whose duties are to receive incoming material, verify the quantity, assign a location, enter the item part number of the item received, the quantity, and the assigned location into the database either manually or the use of scanners, and then store the material in the assigned location safely. The results of the study revealed that the 12 employees in this department worked 50% of the time. One cannot conclude that since 50% of 12 is 6, only 6 employees are needed to fulfill all the duties required. The studies only reveal that fewer than 12 are needed.

The author recommends that a meeting be held to present the results of the studies with the employees, management, the union representative if the employees are represented, and the engineer who conducted the studies. The solution indicates that there is an excessive number of employees in the unloading crew. In the opinion of the author, it is preferred to start with the fewest number of employees to reassign. Then after the change occurs, another work sampling study needs to be conducted to confirm the initial study or to initiate a new one. Based on the author's experience, the utilization rate should range between 60% and 80%. If a reduction in the crew size is indicated, then a request for volunteers be made to transfer to another department. The request for volunteers is the most ethical solution to resolve this situation.

3.6.3 Group timing techniques

This technique employs work sampling techniques that are applied to numerous activities simultaneously so one observer can make an elemental time study that is very detailed for a short interval work sampling procedure for as many as 15 operators and as few as 2. Operator rating is not considered due to the continuous observations being made at fixed predetermined intervals, which tends to level the rating at 100% [9].

3.6.4 Predetermined time systems

Each of these motions is given a predetermined standard time value or a previously fixed time value in such a way that the individual motions are used for total time. These times are summed to yield the normal time to perform a designated task.

1. The use of a default time system requires that the measurement is divided into basic movements/motions, as required by the particular system. All programs must be followed exactly by their own unique rules and procedures.

The most recently developed motion time measurement systems (MTM) is the Most work measurement system. These systems include BasicMost, MiniMost, and MaxiMost [10].

3.6.5 Input from employees

In the opinion of the author, this is the least reliable means of collecting information that will be used for the purpose of measuring the time of manufacturing and costing your product. The reasons are that although the author used three different estimates, they are still estimates; if you are to be judged or held accountable to a number, then you will give a relatively high number, one that you can easily achieve. The negative effects of this method are that the use of materials requirements planning (MRP) will result in inventory being shipped too soon, and the direct cost of manufacturing can be grossly overstated.

3.7 What Are Some Applications of Direct Labor Standards?

1. Direct labor standard hours are used to compute direct labor standard-costs for a process.
2. Direct labor standard labor hours are used to calculate the capacity of a process, production line, or an entire plant.
3. It can be used as a basis for continuous improvement teams.
4. It is used to calculate standard direct variance.

The direct labor variance measures the difference between the actual costs and the standard costs. A positive value indicates that actual costs exceeded standard costs or an unfavorable situation; a favorable situation would exist if actual costs were equal to or less than standard costs [11].

5. It can serve as a basis for the allocation of overhead; another basis for overhead allocation is machine hours.

3.8 What Are Some of the Factors That Affect the Calculation of Productivity or Any KPI?

The purpose of computing productivity or any KPI is to determine progress toward a goal and the effects of changes made in processes, training, etc.

3.8.1 Ethical data collection and standardized definitions of inputs and outputs

1. The collection of data, the methods used in its analysis, the interpretation, and the application of results must be performed in an ethical manner.

    A conclusion can only be made after the collection of data or the conclusion of experiments. As stated by Albert Einstein, "If we knew what we were doing, it would not be called research, would it?"

    As Thomas Sowell stated, "When you want to help people, you tell them the truth. When you want to help yourself, you tell them what they want to hear" [12].

    An example of adjusting input data to obtain a desired goal is the scandal referred to as 'Dieselgate'. This term was applied to the illegal use of a software by Volkswagen to enable their vehicles to pass the emission control standards established by the US Environmental Protection Agency. The US regulations were more strict than those in Europe. The software activated the emission control system only while the vehicle was stationary since vehicles were tested while stationary. During normal operation, the emission control system was turned off and there was no emission control.

Figure 3.3   A large spoon.

The consequences of this action included the allocation of $7.27 billion in 2015 to address the issue, the suspension of all sales in the US of the four-cylinder diesel engine, the loss of 35% of its stock value, a potential fine of up to $37,500 for each vehicle sold with this software, the suspension of several managers, and the loss of customer trust [13].

2. The data must be accurate and the methods used to obtain the data must comply with existing standards and procedures.

3. The standardization and consistency of definitions for inputs and outputs.

An example is the crash of the Mars Climate Orbiter Spaceship in September 1999, which was the result of the contractor, Lockheed-Martin, using English units for its calculations and the expectation by the NASA team that the units would be in metric units. The cost of the mission was $125 million [14].

4. Clearly identified requirements in specifications.

The picture of a large spoon is an example of the need to be specific in the statement of requirements. The customer requested a large spoon and the picture above represents what he received [15].

Another example occurred while managing a project initiated by a technician. The project was to install a healing garden for veterans. The technician requested that the color of the concrete pad be green to stimulate grass. Prior to pouring the concrete, the contractor asked the technician for the specific color of green. This omission resulted in a delay and cost overruns in the project. The technician should have referred to a specific pantone color. Color panels specifying unique colors were available in the adjacent paint shop or in any hardware store.

3.8.2 *The selection and hiring of employees*

A manager who hires employees has not only the responsibility of ensuring that a candidate has the requisite experience, education, and personality but also must be acutely knowledgeable of the ethical aspects of the potential new employee since a main responsibility of management is ethics. Ethics is a personal as well as an organizational issue. Hiring ethical employees is critical for the organization [16].

Managers who do not develop, install, and provide oversight for systems that prevent unethical business practices or fail to provide proper ethical leadership are as much to blame as the individuals who think of, carry out, and benefit knowingly from corporate misbehavior. It is imperative that managers intensify relationships and reputations on which the existence of their organizations relies.

As an example, in the Beech-Nut corporation, then owned by Nestlé, the then CEO realized that the main ingredient in their 100% pure apple juice was a combination of sugar and assorted chemicals. The CEO was under extreme pressure to produce a profit which prevented the disposal of excess inventory and removal of the product from the market. Although numerous employees questioned the purity of the juice from the supplier, the lower costs of this juice enabled the company to meet the goals of cost control. The existing supplier was 25% less than the next lowest competition. A member of the research department who expressed concerns to higher management was deemed to be affected by being naive and having impractical ideals. The sale of a misbranded product was not thought of by anyone to be a legal offense.

Beech-Nut pleaded guilty in 1987 to ten counts of mislabeling the product. The total costs, including fines, lost sales, and legal expenses, were approximately $25 million.

Failures like this usually do not indicate an organizational culture intent on inflicting harm or to be deceptive but one that does not have an effective ethical organizational system [17].

3.8.3 Training of new and existing employees

The backbone of any organization is its employees. The purpose of training is to seal the void between existing levels of performance and the desired level. The Business Dictionary defines training as "an organized activity aimed at imparting information and/or instructions to improve the recipients knowledge or to help him attain a required level of knowledge or skill" [18, 19].

Organizations are successful due to the knowledge and skill level of employees who are the backbone of any organization. Due to the deterioration and obsolescence of skills over time, organizations must provide training and development continuously. Appropriate training must include all levels of employees to include management, sales, supervisors, and technical employees. Employee training is an organized method that can take many forms, as in person or in a classroom, that continually develops employees, increases their and increase the quality of new and existing employees. Training also encourages employees to increase their commitment to their jobs and is essential to increased productivity [20].

Training ensures that each employee understands their role and the optimum methodology to achieve their tasks, but proper training will reduce the likelihood of mistakes, accidents and near misses, and interruptions in production. Cross-training is an excellent method to reduce bottlenecks and increase production. A critical factor in training is ensuring that the correct employee is selected for a particular task. This was the cornerstone of scientific management as proposed by Frederick Taylor [21].

Training should also include work ethics. Work ethics are based on the principle that success will result due to hard work and dedication to the organization and to job performance. Implied in a good work ethic is that the employee will employ excellent and high moral standards both on and off the job. Attributes such as punctuality, organization of your work, the desire of producing exceptional quality, and respect for others are included in the definition of an employee with good work ethics [22].

Although spending for training and development per employee has been reduced from $1,282 in 2019 to $1,111 in 2020, or a 13% reduction due to the pandemic, the following results of a corporate survey of training information reveal that training has a major impact as can be seen in the following statistics:

A. Over two-thirds of employees (68%) believe that training and development is the most important policy.
B. A 24% greater profit exists in organizations that invest in training and development.
C. The retention rate of employees increases by 30–50% for organizations that have rigorous training and development programs.

The failure of employers to provide adequate training programs has adverse effects as indicated below:

A. The costs of less effective training and development programs are estimated to be $13.5 million per 1,000 employees.
B. Almost three-fourths of employees (74%) believe that their inability to realize their full potential is due to the non-existence of training program.
C. Over half (59%) of employees indicated that no formal training program exists for their current position [23].

The commitment to one's job is associated with a positive attitude as that employee performs the assigned tasks and services. It also incorporates the degree of responsibility that the employee has toward the mission and goal of his employer. A committed employee tends to perform his job in such a manner that the goals of the organization are more likely to be realized [24].

3.8.4 The level of involvement, work-related attitudes, and leadership

Job involvement is an indication of the degree to which the job is important to the identity of that employee. From the standpoint of the company, it plays an important role in increasing employee motivation and the increase in productivity. From the standpoint of the employee, it has a huge role in the motivation of the employee, his performance, his personal and professional growth, and his satisfaction. Job involvement increases individual performance due to encouraging them to extend additional effort, creativity, and intelligence in the solution of problems [25].

The results of a study concluded that the motivation of the employee is positively related to performance [26].

These results were corroborated by a study of banking employees in Nigeria which demonstrated a positive correlation at the 0.05 level of significance between employee motivation and productivity [27].

3.8.5 Product design

Proper product design will eliminate unnecessary components and the elimination of unneeded tasks resulting in reduced material, labor, and inventory costs and simultaneously increasing manufacturing throughput. For additional detail, see [28].

3.8.6 Technology and investment of capital

Technology is defined by John Kennedy Galbraith, the Warburg Professor of Economics at Harvard, as "the systematic application of scientific or other organized knowledge to practical tasks". It is defined as the "application of knowledge to the practical aims or human life or on to the change and manipulation of the human environment" [29].

Some of the major changes in technology have happened drastically over time as illustrated in Table 3.3.

Growth of technology spending in actual dollars in the United States over the most recent period can be seen in Table 3.4.

This data can be seen in Figure 3.4. This data is highly correlated as indicated by the R factor of 0.9899.

During the period 2008–2017, private sector spending in various sectors increased from a low of 16.1% to a high of 48.1%.

The only sector that suffered a reduction was mining 11.2%. The sectors and percentage changes can be seen in Table 3.5. [31].

As can be seen in the tables and figure, investment spending, money used to purchase a variety of products intended for long-term gain, has increased. To survive, companies must continue to invest in the future. This investment can be in the form of physical assets, machinery, plant equipment or facilities, employee training, and benefits.

Table 3.3   An Example of Major Changes in Technology over Time [30]

Event	Time of Occurrence
Irrigation	6000 BCE
Sailing	4000 BCE
Iron	1200 BCE
Gunpowder	850 BCE
Windmill	950
Compass	1044
Mechanical clock	1250–1300
Printing	1455
Steam engine	1765
Railways	1804
Steamboat	1807
Photography	1826–1827
Reaper	131
Telegraph	1844
Telephone	1876
Internal combustion engine	1876
Electric lights	1879
Automobiles	1855
Radio	1901
Airplanes	1903
Rocketry	1926
Television	1927
Computer	1937
Nuclear power	1942
Transistor	1947
Spaceflight	1957
Personal computer	1974
Internet	1974
Crisper method of editing genes	2012
Artificial Intelligence	2017

Table 3.4   The Growth of Technology Spending in Actual Dollars Shown in tabular form [31]

Year	$ (Billions)
2012	1230
2013	1258
2014	1311
2015	1449
2016	1507
2017	1582
2018	1681
2019	1793
2020	1832
2021	1943
2022 (est)	2075

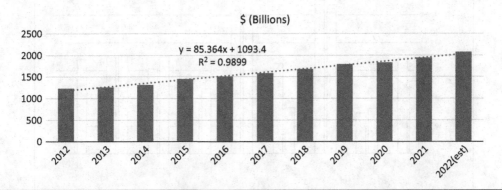

Figure 3.4   The Growth of technology spending in actual dollars shown graphically [29]. The R square value of 0.9899 represents an excellent correlation of technology spending and elapsed time [29].

3.8.7 Machinery and equipment

The term 'machinery and equipment' includes all machinery and equipment used by a manufacturer to produce a product or provide a service [31].

The employment of machines and various types of equipment has produced many benefits in our everyday lives. Some of these include increased productivity, standardization of products, improved utilization of natural

Table 3.5   Percent and Dollar Changes in Sector Spending [31]

Sector	Percent Change	Dollar Change (Billions)
Finance and insurance	26.1	34.6
Health care and social assistance	16.2	14.6
Information	53.5	55.3
Manufacturing	16.5	32.5
Real Estate- Rental and leasing	48.1	51.4
Retail trade	23.4	18.6
Transportation and warehousing	35.0	30.5
Utilities	35.5	35
Wholesale trade	34.0	11.0

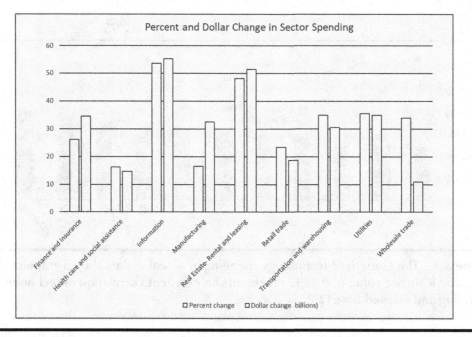

Figure 3.5   Percent and dollar changes in sector spending [31].

resource, the development of roads and other infrastructure needs, a reduction in labor costs, a reduction in the injuries due to poor ergonomics, increased quality of goods and services in a decrease in delivery time, and increased availability of goods [32].

3.9 Examples to Illustrate the Criticality of Ethical Leadership

3.9.1 An automobile dealership

The author worked summers for an automobile dealership that employed four service writers. Each would write requests for various types of services, such as oil and filter change, tire rotation, repair transmission, etc. Since there was no coordination among the service writers, there could be more orders for services that could be performed that day due to time and staff limitations. Productivity for each service was measured by the number of cars served for each day. There were two technicians who performed oil and filter changes, and at the end of each day, the number of vehicles serviced by each was posted for comparison purposes. The problem with this comparison is that the time required for each service varied with a vehicle due to the location of the oil filter, the location of the vehicle to be serviced, and the type of service desired. Some customers wanted just an oil change and some with an oil and filter change. Due to the lack of communication and coordination among the service writers, the number of orders written for this service exceeded the capability of the two technicians.

As the workday was ending, the two technicians would locate vehicles that were scheduled for oil changes and initiate the work orders as if the service had been performed since each service technician received an hourly wage plus incentive pay which was based on the amount of the revenue generated daily. This was done with the full knowledge of the company to avoid customer complaints and to increase revenue. The logic that was employed by the company to justify unethical practice was that the required service was likely to be performed on the next visit. The author was advised by his father who had many years of seniority to maintain silence to enable them to retain their jobs.

This practice achieved several goals:

1. It resulted in an increase in productivity as reported to management. Productivity in this situation was defined as the reported number of services performed per technician per hour, the number of services performed that were reported daily and could not be verified due to a lack of control in the reporting system. The denominator, the number of hours worked, was easily verifiable from the time clock. This is one of the numerous methods of cooking the books, and proper

management controls must be installed to prevent this level of dishonesty. This practice was initiated by management to receive recognition and bonuses. The participating employees did not reveal to customers that some of the services that were paid were services not received due to fear of reprisal and the additional incentive pay received.
2. It resulted in increased revenue for the company and earnings for the technicians.

The proper method to resolve this situation would require the following steps:

a. Determine the mean time required for each type of service using one appropriate technique. Due to the variety of types of cars serviced, the author would have selected work sampling since this method provides accurate times faster than other methods. This situation dictated solutions soon to prevent the continuation of this practice.
b. Calculate the maximum number of services that could be performed daily using the time for the type of service that is greater. The use of the greater time is recommended since this will provide the operator with additional time should an emergency occur, as a stripped drain plug.
c. Assign one or two service technicians to schedule this service and assign a sequential number from 1 to X, where X represents the maximum number of vehicles that can receive those services daily.
d. Place a sign with the assigned number on top of the car for easy location.
e. Evaluate existing pay levels for service technicians with similar duties in similar facilities.
f. Adjust the pay scale without incentive pay so that it exceeds the mean to reward the existing technicians to reward them for loyalty and service.

The issues with this practice were that it was not only unethical but also illegal since many customers paid for services not received. Another concern was that the engines of the cars not actually serviced could suffer potential damage and eventual internal engine damage, depending on how soon the car actually received services that were paid for.

3.9.2 Cooking the books

A practice often referred to as 'cooking the books' is a slang term that refers to the use of various accounting maneuvers by companies that result in the financial situation appearing to be better than its actuality. An example includes the reporting of some expenses in the following quarter resulting in increased earnings for the initial period [33].

This practice is not only illegal and unethical but can result in fines, loss of jobs, bankruptcy, and prison terms, which will be illustrated with the following example.

The Securities and Exchange Commission (SEC) began investigating Under-Armour in 2015 for a practice known as "pulling forward sales". This was done because the company was unable to meet expected revenues for a period, and as a result, pulled forward sales for six months for orders to be shipped in future months. The amount of sales that was pulled forward was $408 million. Advancing sales from future sales to the current period would increase the uncertainty of future sales. This action resulted in a fine by SEC for failure to disclose this action and a class action lawsuit by the stockholders. The stockholders then filed a class action lawsuit against the company for failure to disclose the real reason for the growth in sales and that the company was being investigated by both the SEC and the Department of Justice [34].

References

1. Mahnoor, N.I. (2020). Definition, classification, improve industrial productivity. Retrieved 9/11/2020 from: https://engineerexperiences.com/industrial -productivity.html#:~:text=Definition%20of%20Industrial%20Productivity%3A %20It%20is%20measurement%20the,words%2C%20It%20is%20ratio%20of %20output%20to%20input
2. Rakar, A., Zorzut, S., and Jovan, V. (2004). Assessment of production performance by means by KPI. Jozef Stefan Institute. Control. Univ of Bath, UK. Sep 2004. Retrieved 2/24/2022 from: http://portal.sabalift.com/Portals/6/%D8%A2 %D9%85%D9%88%D8%B2%D8%B4/ASSESMENT%20OF%20PRODUCTION %20PERFORMANCE%20BY%20MEANS%20OF%20KPI.pdf
3. Picture of paper tubes with one end turned in or crimped. Retrieved 3/11/2022 from: https://www.google.com/search?q=free+picture+of+paper+tube+yarn +carrier&sxsrf=ALiCzsaL7xWGcQYOWMHSi5oejOyNXiKG7A%3A1664321411108 &source=hp&ei=g4czY6mGA7-zqtsPxc6ngA4&iflsig=AJiK0e8AAAAAYzOVkwh

heGIhN1IuOMdTyezPmoM3J0KR&ved=0ahUKEwjp0_2zkLb6AhW_mWoF-
HUXnCeAQ4dUDCA8&oq=free+picture+of+paper+tube+yarn+carrier&gs_lcp
=Cgdnd3Mtd2l6EAwyBQghEKABMgUIIRCgAToHCCMQ6gIQJzoECCMQJzo

4. Energy productivity, energy productivity playbook: Alliance to save energy.
Retrieved 7/28/2022 from: https://www.ase.org/sites/ase.org/files/gaep
_playbook-energy-productivity_alliance-to-save-energy.pdf#:~:text=ENERGY
%20PRODUCTIVITY%20is%20a%20measure%20of%20the%20economic,of
%20oil%20equivalent%2C%20or%20kilowatt%20hours%20of%20electricity%29

5. Bazerman, M. (2020). A new model for ethical leadership. *Harvard Business
Review*, Sep–Oct. Retrieved 8/22/2020 from: https://hbr.org/2020/09/a-new
-model-for-ethical-leadership

6. Picture of upholstered chair with brass nail trim. Retrieved 9/11/2022 from:
https://www.freepik.com/premium-photo/old-brown-leather-sofa-close-up
_6687300.htm#query=pictures%20of%20upholstered%20chairs%20with
%20brass%20nail%20trim&position=30&from_view=search&track=ais

7. Watson, G.J. and Derouin, J. (2022). *Integration of Methods Improvement and
Measurement into Industrial Engineering Functions*. CRC Press, Boca Raton,
FL, ISBN 978-0367-72093.

8. Work Sampling. (n.d.). Retrieved 1/21/2021 from: https://www.businessman
agementideas.com/production-management/techniques/work-sampling
-objectives-theory-and-applications/7244\

9. Brisley, C.L. (2001) *Sampling and Group Timing Technique. Maynard's
Industrial Engineering Handbook*. 5th edition. McGraw Hill, New York, pp.
17.47–17.64.

10. Zandin, K.B. (2001). *Most@Work Measurement Systems. Maynards
Industrial Engineering Handbook*. 5th edition. McGraw Hill, New York, pp.
17.65–17.82.

11. Definition of direct labor variance. Retrieved 8/11/2022 from: https://www
.cfajournal.org/direct-labor-rate-variance/#:~:text=Variance%20Analysis
%20Definition%3A%20Direct%20Labor%20rate%20variance%20indicates
,between%20the%20actual%20and%20expected%20cost%20of%20labor

12. Goodreads. (n.d.). Retrieved 5/22/2022 from: https://www.goodreads.com
/author/quotes/2056.Thomas_Sowell

13. Kabey, M.J.B. (2019). Corporate governance in manufacturing and management with analysis of governance failures at Enron and Volkswagen corporations. *American Journal of Operations Management and Information
Systems*, 4(4), 109–123. Retrieved 1/26/2023 from: https://www.researchgate
.net/profile-MosesKabeyi/publication/338489019_Corporate_Governance_in
_Manufacturing_and_Management_with_Analysis_of_Governance_Failures
_at_Enron_and_Volkswagen_Corporations/links/5e414f7292851c7f7f2c5b2b
/Corporate-Governance-in-Manufacturing-and-Management-with-Analysis-of
-Governance-Failures-at-Enron-and-Volkswagen Retrieved 1/22/2023 from:
https://spacemath.gsfc.nasa.gov/weekly/6Page53.pdfCorporations.pdf?_sg%5B0
%5D=started_experiment_milestone&origin=journalDetail

14. Some famous conversion errors. Retrieved 1/22/2023 from: https://www
.bing.com/search?q=Some%20Famous%20Conversion%20Errors.&qs=n&form
=QBRE&=%25eManage%20Your%20Search%20History%25E&sp=-1&pq=some
%20famous%20conversion%20errors.&sc=10-30&sk=&cvid=CF8BC9DDCC1
34B05A778F6AC366CF015&ghsh=0&ghacc=0&ghpl=

15. A large spoon. Retrieved 1/27/2021 from: I received a comedically large spoon:
funny (reddit.com)

16. Villegas, S., Lloyd, R.A., Tritt, A., and Vengrouskie, E.F. (2019). Human
resources as ethical gatekeepers: Hiring ethics and employee selection.
Journal of Leadership, Accountability and Ethics. Retrieved 8/5/2022 from:
https://d1wqtxts1xzle7.cloudfront.net/84389660/1924-with-cover-page-v2.pdf
?Expires=1665430133&Signature=ZLnF5Ts~bE6ku2iOVnne7aua0Q6ZPBKgA3C
~ZWfhne0WPc5rw-YJh0mgc8Rj2Jg0iOcDTu7IrQg6mMcFYaQEseuDhJou9Swte
AjnvBrVh~lhtUONEhmYDZ6MiiCDegX7HNgx67UkIgwogKPZBOQXtc5GW
U6GV0OMEb1bVj6CJGzNFK2uO3sDgMx7tjiVDS~JGQMaHhncyVjT8cErMpEsVX
WUsdCHb8Kqx2DXkLwfQ8j4f0vTlm10zQlOIvIDGoOH1rZJN2Q2Ou7NKQP0zq
8AmnTJ0KAVXg6xajyDxQTwk6guEJU1ZkV1JSRohfF5qWcH0j31yHxq8wYgIa
ntSPp7BQ__&Key-Pair-Id=APKAJLOHF5GGSLRBV4ZA

17. Paine, L.S. (1994). Managing for organizational integrity. *Harvard Business
Review*, Mar–Apr. Retrieved 8/5/2022 from: https://hbr.org/1994/03/managing
-for-organizational-integrity

18. The Business Dictionary. (n.d.). Retrieved 5/12/2022 from: http://www
.businessdictionary.com/definition/training.html#ixzz361jeoyTo

19. Noe, R.A. (n.d.). *Employee Training and Development.* 5th edition. McGraw-
Hill, New York. ISBM 978-0-07-353034-5. Retrieved 6/11/2022 from: https://
www.academia.edu/37724770/Employee_Training_and_Development_book

20. Halawi, A., and Haydar, N. (2018). Effects of training on employee performance: A case study of Bonjus and Khatib and Alumni Companies.
International Humanities Studies, 5(2). ISSN 2311-7796. Retrieved 11/18/2021
from: https://www.researchgate.net/publication/260219097

21. Nda, M.M., and Fard, R.Y. (2013). The impact of employee training and
development on employee productivity. *Global Journal of Commerce and
Management Perspective*, Nov–Dec 2013. ISSN-2319-7285. Retrieved 6/21/2022
from: https://www.researchgate.net/publication/260219097_THE_IMPACT
_OF_EMPLOYEE_TRAINING_AND_DEVELOPMENT_ON_EMPLOYEE
_PRODUCTIVITY

22. Indeed Editorial Team. (2021). Work ethics and success in the workplace.
Retrieved 6/11/2021 from: https://ca.indeed.com/career-advice/career
-development/work-ethi

23. Employee training statistics-cost of progress in 2022. Retrieved 9/12/2022
from:https://teautmstage.io/training-statistics/A

24. Business Courses. (n.d.). Job commitment and overview. Retrieved 7/11/2022
from: https://study.com/academy/lesson/job-commitment-definition-lesson-quiz
.html

25. Psychology - industrial organizational psychology - work motivation - job involvement. Retrieved 3/5/2022 from: https://psychology.iresearchnet.com/industrial-organizational-psychology/work-motivation/job-involvement/#:~:text=From%20an%20individual%20perspective%2C%20job%20involvement%20constitutes%20a,and%20making%20it%20a%20meaningful%20and%20fulfilling%20experience

26. Ryanoto, S., Endri, E., and Herlisisha, N. (2021). Effect of work motivation on employee performance. *Problems and Perceptions in Management*, 19(3), 162–174. Retrieved 7/11/2022 from: https://www.researchgate.net/profile/Setyo Riyanto/publication/354034008_Effect_of_work_motivation_and_job _satisfaction_on_employee_performance:Mediating_role_of_employee _engagement. n\ks/61249c78a8348b1a46ff48ea/Effect-of-work-motivation-and -job-satisfaction-on-employee-performance-Mediating-role-of-employee -engagement.pdf

27. Ifeoluwa Ajijola Inioluwa Aderibigbe. (2017). Relationship between employee motivation and productivity among bankers in Nigeria. *Journal of Economics*, 8(1), 76–80. Retrieved 7/22/2022 from: https://www.tandfonline.com/action /showCitFormats?doi=10.1080%2F09765239.2017.1316964

28. Zhou, A., and Watson, G.J. (2022). *Applied Engineering Design*, Kendall Hunt Publishing Company, Dubuque. ISBN-978–1-7924-9912-8

29. Marglin, S., Parker, R., Sen, A., and Friedman, F. (Chr). (2008). John Kenneth Galbraith. *The Harvard Gazette*. Retrieved 4/22/2022 from: https://www.bing .com/search?q=definition%20of%20techology&form=SWAUA2

30. Gregersen, E. (n.d.). History of technology timeline. *Britannica*. Retrieved 6/11/2022 from: https://www.britannica.com/story/history-of-technology -timeline

31. Business and government spending on information and business technology in the United States from 2012 to 2022. (n.d.). Retrieved 4/22/2022 from: https://www.statista.com › statistics › 821769 › us

32. Seth, T. (n.d.). Economics discussion, the advantages and disadvantages of the use of machinery. Retrieved 2/27/2022 from: https://www.economicsdiscussion .net/articles/advantages-and-disadvantages-of-the-use-of-machinery/1545

33. Kenton, W. (2021). *Cook the Books*. Retrieved 4/11/2022 from: https://www .investopedia.com/terms/c/cookthebooks.asp#:~:text=What%20Is%20%27Cook %20the%20Books%27%3F%20Cook%20the%20books,order%20to%20pump %20up%20its%20earnings%20or%20profit.

34. The Litigation Practice Group. (2021). Under-Armour Inc pulls sales forward, SEC and stockholders push back. *The National Law Review*, XI(138). Retrieved 6/16/2022 from: https://www.natlawreview.com/article/under-armour-inc-pulls -sales-forward,SEC -and-Stockholders-Push-Back

Chapter 4

Improved Productivity, Efficiency, and Reduced Downtime

4.1 Requirements for Continual Improvements in Productivity, Efficiency, and Reductions in Downtime Are as Follows:

1. An assessment of the degree of ethical leadership at all levels of management which has been defined as

   leadership demonstrating and promoting normatively appropriate conduct through personal actions and interpersonal relations. [1]

   Ethical leadership is one in which the leaders possess the ability to guide individuals in various decisions involving ethical values such as fairness, morals, honesty, equality, and respect [2].
       The common denominator of the existing definitions of ethical leadership from the literature is the degree to which employees are involved in their jobs. Numerous studies demonstrate a positive correlation between employee engagement and productivity.

2. The determination of the level of employee engagement and then taking of appropriate action to increase it by demonstrating appropriate conduct during relationships between employees, customers, vendors,

DOI: 10.4324/9781003302308-4

and federal and local regulatory agencies. This philosophy can be simply summarized as "the treatment of others as you want to be treated" or "practice what you preach".

Employee engagement was incorporated into management theory in the decade beginning in 2000. Most agree as to the benefits it brings to an organization but not all due to its difficulty to measure. A recent Gallup survey over the period 2000–2018 indicates an increase in employee engagement from approximately 25% to 35%. The survey shows a decrease in the number of actively disengaged employees from approximately 18% to approximately 14% over the same period. Despite its volatility over this period, employee engagement increased during this period [3].

Measurement methods for determining employee engagement include both survey and non-survey techniques. Surveys could be short ones that are frequently sent to employees. Often referred to as pulse surveys, these usually contain fewer than ten questions whose purpose is to obtain feedback on a certain topic. These types of surveys can be sent extemporaneously or at a scheduled interval. These are usually employed to determine employee attitudes or thoughts concerning a specific idea or concept.

Another type of survey is one to garnish the degree of loyalty of your employees to the organization. Usually, the survey consists of only one question, which is to rate on a scale of one to ten the likelihood that you will recommend this organization as a great place to work [4]. Increases in employee engagement are correlated to management engagement. The degree of employee engagement is a measure of the level of devotion and enthusiasm for his job. The focus of an engaged employee is not the salary or wages he receives. He also tends to associate his physical and mental state with his performance, which is vital to the success of the organization.

Engaged employees share the following traits:

A. Have knowledge of their task and the role it plays in the organization.
B. Possess the desire to achieve and exceed expectations.
C. Are productive and loyal to their employer.
D. Are focused on success for themselves and their organization.
E. Are motivated to perform at an ever-increasing level.

To increase employee engagement, the organization should take the following steps:

A. Ensure that all managers are engaged.
B. Establish realistic goals with employees.
C. Ensure open and honest communication between employees and management.
D. Ensure visibility between all levels in the organization to enable any employee to receive assistance and guidance as needed.
E. Provide the necessary resources including new technology.
F. Demonstrate appreciation for accomplishments and contributions.
G. Focus on employee enjoyment as a reward. The next task is to employ one of the many available productivity improvement tools.
H. The installation of a maintenance management program. Critical to the operation of machines and equipment is effective maintenance management. Two maintenance strategies exist: reactive and planned maintenance. If an organization employs the reactive approach, repairs are made only when needed. The best example of reactive maintenance, or unplanned maintenance, occurs when a burnt-out lightbulb is replaced. This type of maintenance is usually employed in organizations that seek maximum output or those that have low investment in reconfiguring manufacturing systems which are simply determining quickly how to manufacture the needed components until the needed repairs are completed on the machine that malfunctioned disrupting production.

For several reasons, such as increased competition, the customer demands for improved quality products, and a reduction in leadtime, maintenance management has realized major changes. The goal of maintenance management is to minimize the negative effects of machine breakdowns and to maximize the availability of equipment at minimum costs.

The objectives of both types of preventative maintenance, preventive and predictive is to minimize unscheduled maintenance and costs due to lost production. Preventive maintenance occurs at regular intervals as specified by the manufacturer. An example is the changing of oil and filter in an automobile at the intervals specified by the manufacturer using the specified materials. Predictive maintenance uses feedback from the equipment operation to determine incremental degradation to predict the optimum time to perform maintenance to reduce costly downtime [5].

The most costly downtime events are an environmental error, an accident or injury, and unscheduled downtime, which include both obvious and hidden costs. The obvious costs of machine downtime include waste, cost of lost production, the quality costs for the detection of defects, and the costs for needed retraining to prevent future downtime occurrences. Less obvious costs include the costs of idle employees, the loss of potential sales, loss of potential revenue, and profit margin.

Unplanned maintenance occurs more frequently than desired. In fact during the most recent three-year period, 82 percent incurred at least one period of disrupted production due to an unplanned breakdown. An average of 800 unplanned hours per year are realized by manufacturers per year. This amount of downtime approximates 15 hours per week.

The results of one study that the four major causes of downtime include:

1. Equipment failure
2. Lack of components
3. An accident or injury
4. The lack of trained personnel

The study also concluded that the majority , 42 percent, of the $50 billion costs attributable to unplanned downtime was due to equipment failure.

The four most common types of breakdowns will assist in the development and management of the appropriate type of maintenance program. Obsolete and dilapidated rather than depreciating since depreciating is usually associated with accounting and not engineering, errors attributable to the operator, incomplete maintenance procedures, and inadequate inspection methods. Recommendations to reduce downtime include operator training, a simple plan for preventive maintenance, the accurate documentation of previous repairs, and maintaining an updated electronic database [6].

Proper maintenance is essential for all equipment regardless of the purpose of the equipment. The avoidance of proper maintenance is not only unethical but can result in undesirable consequences that can be more costly and damaging than the maintenance costs that the company avoided. An excellent example is Pacific Gas and Electric (PG&E). The company was indicted by a Federal Grand Jury for failure to observe safety regulations that resulted in the explosion of a natural gas line in 2010 in San Bruno, California, that destroyed a neighborhood and killed eight people. The company was found guilty by a jury of five safety violations as well as one count of obstruction. Initially, the company faced fines of $562 million which was reduced to $6 million. The company paid out a total exceeding $1.7 billion in fines and restitution. The National Transportation Safety Board and the California Public Utilities Commission faulted the company for lapses in management and their concern to prioritize profits before safety [7].

The lack of an overall safety strategy, precise communications between management and employees in the field concerning safety, and the reactive safety policy were given as primary causes of wildfires in a 2017 report to state regulators. One wildfire, referred to as the Camp Fire, was caused by a transmission tower that was 25 years old but the utility had failed to replace it. More than 1,500 wildfires in California have been caused by PG&E powerlines during the last six years.

A different California utility, the San Diego Gas and Electric, has implemented many changes to reduce the likelihood of a wildfire and to minimize the effects should one occur.

These changes included:

1. A reduction in the size of the power grid that has been enabling the shutoff of power in isolated areas as needed.
2. The clearing of trees and upgrade of equipment.
3. The monitoring of weather conditions at every pole for the potential of fire.
4. The video recording of data across its network.
5. The expenditure of $1.5 billion since 2007 to upgrade and maintain its power lines [8].

4.2 The Establishment of Continuous Improvement Teams

Another readily available tool is continuous improvement teams. These teams must include members from management, maintenance, engineering, and the production area in which increased productivity is sought. The team needs to develop a charter and a means of communication to inform all employees of the mission of the team and its progress toward its goal. The team mission should be focused on one or a few goals, and after achievement, the team should be dissolved and a new team formed as new priorities emerge.

Continuous improvement teams have been employed in a variety of areas with great results. The implementation of a continuous improvement team in an interior case design study achieved the following results:

1. A turnaround reduction of projects from 16 to 9 weeks or an improvement of 44 percent
2. An increased profit margin from 25 to 27 percent for a 4 percent improvement
3. The percentage of proposal that were accepted from 11 to 32 percent or an improvement of 191 percent [9].

Table 4.1 An Example of a W3I

Team Name	Hand Sanding				Date 7/3/2022
Mission	To evaluate three brands of 180-grit sandpaper to determine the brand that is the least expensive to use in the Hand Sanding Department				
Team members	Bill A	Susan S	Michael W	Marvin M	
Who	What				When
Team members	Select brands to test				8/27/2022
Team members	Develop testing procedures				
Team member	Define the least expensive to use				
Team members	Conduct tests				
Team members	Evaluate results				
Team members	Make recommendation				
Engineer representative	Initiate ECO				

One proven method of communication familiar to the author uses an Excel spreadsheet referred to as a W3I. The three Ws represent who, what, and why. The "I" was for "information".

An example can be seen below.

4.3 The Implementation of Lean Manufacturing

The beginning of lean manufacturing began with the Toyota Production System (TPS) which has changed over time. The TPS came into existence due to the need to compete with the American automobile industry. The efficiencies of the American automobile industry depended on large lot production due to long set-up times. Ford Motor Company, under the guidance of Henry Ford, implemented a number of practices, such as interchangeable components, the standardization of work, and the assembly line that resulted in high-speed production of products. One disadvantage of this system was that it was not flexible. To illustrate this flaw, the model T was manufactured with few changes for 19 years. Model T was the only product that was produced on that assembly line. Since the model T was the only product manufactured on that line, there was no need for changeovers or setups of equipment [10].

After the conclusion of WWII, the president of the Toyota Motor Company, Toyoda Kiichiro, advised the Japanese automobile industry to "Catch up with the Americans in three years" or the Japanese automobile industry will not survive. This was attributable to the fact that the American worker produced about nine times the products and components than the Japanese worker. The greater productivity in the American automobile industry was partly attributable to large production quantities due to the long set-up times. Since the demand for the products of the Japanese auto industry was less than the demand for products of the American auto industry, the production of large quantities to offset long set-up times was not possible.

The focus of the TPS is the elimination of waste. The basis of the TPS system is a process referred to as the "5 whys", a process which will eventually result in the real cause of the problem. For example, an operator at the Toyota textile plant could efficiently operate 40–45 looms whereas an operator at the Toyota automobile plant could operate only one machine at a time. The "5 whys" process determined that the reason for this difference was that, unlike the looms at the Toyota Textile plant, the machines at the Toyota automobile plant did not stop at the end of the process. The first step in the installation of the TPS was to redesign the plant based on the flow of the product through the plant. The next step was to replace the concept of one operator for each process with one operator, many processes. This resulted in an increase in productivity of at least 100%.

To illustrate the benefits and methodology of implementing this concept, the author worked at a furniture plant that employed a computer numerically controlled (CNC) router that would produce components for a chair, settee, or sofa based on the program. The process was to place a 5 ft × 10 ft × 25 mm sheet of plywood onto the bed of the machine with the assistance of a pneumatic lift. Then after proper placement of the plywood onto the bed, the operator would initiate the program that would route the components as dictated. After completing the program, the operator would manually remove the components and place them onto an adjacent cart for assembly. Production of the components would require from 6 to 10 minutes depending on the number and complexity of the components.

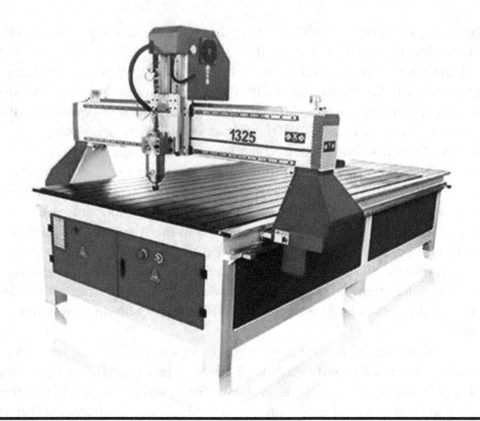

Figure 4.1   A CNC router [12].

After the removal of the parts from the bed of the machine, the operator would remove any remaining saw dust with an attached vacuum hose. This the operator incurred unforced idle time during the operation of the router [11].

The situation was discussed with the existing and future potential operator and was advised that utilizing the unforced idle time to operate another machine would be advantageous to the company and to the operator himself. The operator agreed and was then asked which additional task was possible during the operation of the CNC router (see Figure 4.1).

The operator provided several suggestions, and a decision was made to relocate a small two-headed sander adjacent to the CNC router. The steps involved in the operation of this sander were to remove and properly position eight curved plywood backs from a hand cart onto the bed of the machine and depress the start button, The backs would then be automatically fed into the sander one at a time, and positioned for removal from the sander onto another hand cart.

T represents the transportation of people, material, inventory, and information.

I represents inventory which includes both raw materials, work in process, and finished goods. Also included is damaged or obsolete material, work in process or finished goods, or outdated or obsolete information.

M represents movement, which could encompass people, material, and information.

W represents waiting, which includes waiting for information, people, and material.

O represents overproduction and refers to the manufacture of products or work in process that is not required and is stored in inventory.

Another O represents overprocessing and refers to the addition of features or attributes to a product that is not requested by the customer.

Defects are products, materials, or information that do not meet the customer's requirements.

Skills refer to the underutilized capabilities of employees or the assignment of tasks to people that do not possess the needed training.

Just in time manufacturing (JIT) is one of the many provisions of lean manufacturing. The author fully embraces the concept with limitations as explained in the following examples.

The author worked for a furniture manufacturer that employed Manufacturing Resource Planning (MRP) to order and scheduled the receipt of purchased components. Due to its bulkiness, the plant ordered and scheduled foam so that it could be removed from the trailer and carried directly to the production cell to prevent excessive motion of the foam. Prior to this change, the foam was removed from the delivery trailer, received into inventory, inspected, stored temporarily, and then taken to a designated work cell when needed.

This change decreased the indirect labor costs of temporary storage and inspection upon receipt. Inspection was now conducted by the operators, one of the tenets of lean manufacturing.

Foam deliveries occurred two times a day, one early in the morning for the production scheduled that morning and one later that day at lunch for the production scheduled that afternoon [13].

Theoretically, this situation eliminated the excessive travel time of the foam and reduced indirect labor costs. Although the team that initiated this improvement was engaged in the project and led by ethical management, the one missing component to increase the likelihood of a successful implementation was the lack of critical thinking. In a previous work by the author titled *Critical*

Thinking-Learning from Mistakes and How to Prevent Them, the author ana-
lyzed 33 mistakes he had made and observed the causes of mistakes. A graphi-
cal depiction of causes of Mistakes can be seen in Figure 4.2 and Table 4.2 [14].

During the decision-making process, due to the lack of critical thinking, one critical aspect of the project was not taken into consideration – the
omitted consideration was asking the question – "What is the worst that can
happen?" For this situation, the worst was the inability to deliver the foam as
scheduled due to a truck malfunction. The delivery vehicle ran out of gasoline to the manufacturer.

The result of non-delivery resulted in the temporary shutdown of the
plant due to the lack of foam, which is one of the least expensive components used in the manufacture of furniture. The temporary suspension of

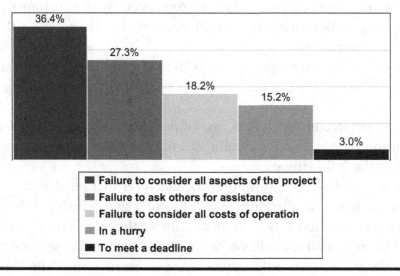

Figure 4.2   Distribution of mistakes by cause category [15].

Table 4.2   Frequency Distribution of Causes of Mistakes

Reasons for mistakes	Percentage	Number of errors
Failure to consider all aspects of the project	36.4	12
Failure to ask others for assistance	27.3	9
Failure to consider all costs of operation	18.2	6
In a hurry	15.2	5
To meet a deadline	3.0	1
Total of all mistakes	100.0	33

production resulted in late deliveries, unsatisfied furniture customers, and late or no payment.

The solution required the vendor to have a secondary delivery vehicle if needed and a real-time communication system between the vendor, the driver, and the customer.

Another costly mistake occurred because the material planner was in a hurry to make a decision and place an order for a specialty leather due to lead time for the leather, which was purchased from a foreign distant vendor. The leather was to be used to upholster some chairs that were to be used in the chairman's conference room in a distant state. The leather was to match the color of the carpet from a domestic manufacturer. The material planner sent a JPEG image of the carpet to the leather vendor.

In order to maintain this large customer, all the chairs had to be replaced at the customer's location to enable the conference room to be used. The material planner first ordered a square yard of the carpet with the same Pantone color for the carpet, and sent it via airfreight to the leather vendor. The vendor was instructed to airfreight four hides of this color each week to the end customer's address until notified and inform the planner upon shipment. The chair manufacturer then scheduled four employees – a leather cutter, a sewer, an upholsterer, and an assembly person – each week to fly to the end-user on a Monday and return the following Friday until all the chairs had been upholstered, a process that required four weeks. Accommodations including meals and a car rental were also provided to these employees. In addition to these out-of-pocket costs, the manufacturer incurred numerous overtime hours for the remaining employees due to the absence of those who repaired the chairs due to the color variation. Upon completion, the furniture manufacturer apologized for the delay and confusion and offered the chairs at no cost to compensate. Although this decision was costly and resulted in a loss, this decision was proper and ethical since the furniture manufacturer was more interested in its reputation and long-term sales and profit than short-term gains.

4.4 The Implementation of Additive Manufacturing (AM) Where Feasible

Additive manufacturing, or 3D printing, resulted from changes made to an inkjet printer. Additive manufacturing , a process that adds material, differs from normal manufacturing processes that remove material. Additive manufacturing, a process that adds material, differs from normal manufacturing processes that remove material. A MIT professor, Dr. Emanual Sachs, introduccd the term, 3D printing in 1995, and is interchangeable with additive manufacturing. Unlike normal manufacturing processes which remove material, additive manufacturing adds material to produce the final product. A modified 3D printer is used with 3D Scanners and CAD (Computer Aided Design Software) to produce or print a product. The advantages of AM include a reduction in lead times, material costs, and the ability to produce a prototype in less time than with traditional manufacturing methods [16].

Solutions to real-time demand exist due to this application. The initial applications of AM or 3D printing were for components in the automobile and aerospace industries. This process enables the rapid production of prototypes enabling testing to insure compliance with needed specifications. Another advantage of this process is the prevention of expenditures that would be required to manufacture this item with the previously used processes which removed material. The process is also employed in the construction of models, which enable architects, engineers, and others to demonstrate plans to clients.

Recent applications have expanded into healthcare and include the printing of prosthetics, dentures, various medical devices such as masks for continuous positive airways pressure (CPAP) and Bilevel positive airway pressure BiPAP machines, accessories such as personal face masks, and buildings that can be used for isolation wards. Bioprinting, a recent proposed advancement, is the use of human tissue to print human organs. The goal is to mitigate the shortage of donor-supplied organs. The material used to print these organs would be tissue from the patient reducing the likelihood of tissue rejection [17].

4.5 The Holding of Kaizen Events

A kaizen event is a workshop occurrence that is dedicated toward a specific purpose in process improvement. The workshop can occur over a period of three to five days. Critical to the success of the event are its members who must possess an excellent understanding of the process to evaluate and be motivated to seek a solution. Planning is crucial and requires a statement of the problem to be studied. Included in the problem statement are the participants, the timing of the event, and the objective.

A kaizen event is similar to a continuous improvement team but exists for a finite time and focuses on an immediate solution to a problem [18].

A. What is the meaning of improvements in productivity, efficiency, and machine downtime?

Increases in productivity, efficiency, and machine downtime mean to do more with less, specifically, it is producing more products or services with fewer resources.

Increases in productivity can be achieved in several ways: an increase in output with no increase in input, output remaining constant with a decrease in input, an increase in both output and input but the percentage increase in output exceeding the percentage increase in input, and conversely, a decrease in both output and input with the decrease in output being less than the decrease in input [19].

An increase in efficiency results when resources are better utilized while a machine is operating. It can be achieved by ensuring that employees are properly trained and that anything that may result in delays is reduced as much as possible. Production standards have allowances, personal time, fatigue, and delay added to accommodate unforeseen circumstances.

A decrease in machine downtime will result in increased productivity because it provides additional time for the process, assembly line, or plant to produce quality products or services. Machine downtime is costly due to lost production and the costs required to enable the process, assembly line, or plant to begin producing quality products and services.

B. Why is increased productivity important?

Productivity increases in all areas result in the production of more goods and services with no increase in the amount of work. Over the

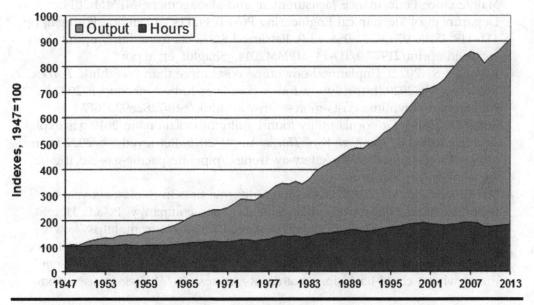

Figure 4.3   Graph of productivity and hours over a 66-year period [20].

period 1947–2013, the US was able to produce nine times more goods and services with a small increase in the number of labor hours. Other advantages include a reduced cost per unit and an increase in throughput (see Figure 4.3).

References

1. Zhang, Y., Zhou, F., and Mao, J. (2018). Ethical leadership and follower moral actions; investigating an emotional linkage. *Frontiers in Psychology*, Oct 4, 2018. Retrieved 8/23/2022 from: https://www.ncbi.nlm.nih.gov/pmc/articles/PMC6180164/

2. Bhasin, H, (2021). Ethical leadership: Definition, meaning, importance, principles and examples. *Marketing*, 91. Retrieved 7/13/2022 from: https://www.marketing91.com/ethical-leadership/#:~:text=Ethical%20leadership%20is%20the%20art%20of%20influencing%20people,teach%20people%20the%20difference%20between%20right%20and%20wrong

3. Pendell, R. (2022). The world's 7.8 trillion workplace problem. Gallup. June 14,2022. Retrieved 8/06/2022 from: https://www.gallup.com/workplace/393497/world-trillion-workplace-problem.aspx#:~:text=Gallup%27s%20most%20recent%20employee%20engagement,18%25%20higher%20productivity%20(sales)5

4. *Qualtrics 2020 Global Employment Experience Trends Report.* (2020). Retrieved 5/18/2022 from: https://www.qualtrics.com/experience-management/employee/measure-employee-engagement/

5. Shagluf, A., Longstaff, A.P., and Fletcher, S. (2014). Maintenance strategies to reduce downtime due to machine positional errors. In: Proceedings of Maintenance Performance Measurement and Management. MPMM 2014. Department of Mechanical Engineering Pólo II FCTUC, Coimbra, Portugal, pp. 111–118. ISBN 978-972-8954-42-0. Retrieved 8/2/2022 from: http://eprints.hud.ac.uk/id/eprint/21977/1/ID-13_MPMM2014,_Shagluf_et_al.pdf

6. Ravande, S. (2022). Unplanned downtime costs more than you think. *Forbes*. Retrieved 8/4/2020: https://www.forbes.com/sites/forbestechcouncil/2022/02/22/unplanned-downtime-costs-more-than-you-think/?sh=7282e92636f7

7. Fuller, T. (2016). California utility found guilty of violations in 2010 gas explosion that killed 8. *The New York Times*, Aug 9, 2016. Retrieved 8/6/2022 from: https://www.phmsa.dot.gov/safety-awareness/pipeline/pacific-gas-electric-pipeline-rpture-san-bruno-ca

8. McFall-Johnsen, M. (2019). Over 1500 California fires in the last six years- including the deadliest ever- were caused by one companyy- PG&E. Here's what it could have done but didn't. Retrieved 7/11/2022 from: https://www.businessinsider.in/science/environment/news/over-1500-california-fires-in-the-last-6-years-including-the-deadliest-ever-were-caused-by-one-company-pge-heres-what-it-could-have-done-but-didnt-/articleshow/71879834.cms#:~:text

=Pacific%20Gas%20%26%20Electric%20Co.%20%28PG%26E%29%20power
%20lines,of%20prioritizing%20profits%20over%20safety%20measures%20for
%20decades

9. Khan, S.A., Kaviani, M.A., Galli, B.J., and Ishtaq, P. (2019). Application of continuous improvement techniques to improve organization performance: A case
study. *International Journal of Lean Six Sigma*. ISSN: 2040-4166. Retrieved
7/21/2022 from: https://scholar.google.com/scholar?hl=en&as_sdt=0%2C5&as
_ylo=2018&q=Khan%2C+S.A%2C+Kaviani%2C%2C+M.+A%2C+Galli.+B.J.%2C
+and+Ishtiaq%2C+Palvisha+%282019%29&btnG=

10. Ciarniene, R., and Vienasindiene, M. (2012). Lean manufacturing: Theory
and practice. Economics and practice. *Economics and Management*, 2012;
17(2). Retrieved 8/1/2022 from: https://www.process.st/lean-manufacturing
-principles/

11. Ohno, T. (1988). *Toyoto Production System; Beyond Large Scale Production*.
CRC Press. Retreived 8/23/2022 from: https://books.google.com/books/about
/Toyota_Production_System.html?id=7_-67SshOy8C

12. Illustration 4.1 an example of a CNC router. Retrieved 7/22/2022 from: https://
www.shutterstock.com/image-photo/wood-cut-industrial-cnc-machine
-1206061720

13. What is additive manufacturing? Definition and processes. (n.d.). Retrieved
1/15/2021 from: https://www.twi-global.com/technical-knowledge/faqs/what-is
-additive-manufacturing

14. Watson, G.J., and Derouin, J.J. (2021). *Critical Thinking- Learning
from Mistakes and How to Prevent Them*. CRC Press, Boca Raton, FL,
ISBN-978–0-367-35460-2.

15. Choon, Y.Y., Tan, H.W., Patel, D.C., Choon, W.T., et al. (2020). The global rise in
3D printing during the covid-19 pandemic. *Nature Reviews Material*, 5, 637–
639. Retrieved 10/30/2020 from: https://www.nature.com/articles/s41578-020
-00234-3

16. Dodziuk, H. (2016). Applications of 3D printing in healthcare. *Polish Journal
of Thoracic and Cardiovascular Surgery*, Sep;13(3). PMID:27785150. Retrieved
11/2/2022 from: https://www.academia.edu/50726225/Applications_of_3D
_printing_in_healthcare

17. What is just in time (JIT) inventory management? Retrieved 8/11/2022 from:
https://www.bing.com/search?q=what+is+jit&form=MSNSB1&refig=f016830a14a
a40389eeab0b9791ceee7&mkt=en-us&ocid=U519DHP&sp=1&qs=HS&pq=what
+is&sk=PRES1&sc=10-7&cvid=f016830a14aa40389eeab0b9791ceee7

18. Overview: What is a kaizen event? Retrieved 7/16/2022 from: https://www.isix-
sigma.com/dictionary/kaizen-event/

19. Mahnoor. (2020). Definition, classification, improve industrial productivity.
Engineer Experiences. Retrieved 5/22/2022 from: https://engineerexperiences
.com/industrial-productivity.html#:~:text=Productivity%20improvement%20is
%20a%20continuous%20process.%20It%20involves,e.g%20cost%20reduction
%2C%20material%20productivity%2C%20waste%20control%20etc

20. Graph of productivity and hours over a sixty six year period. https:// www.bls .gov /k12 /productivity -101 /content /why -is -productivity -important /home.htm#:~ :text =Productivity %20increases %20have %20enabled %20the ,the %20same%20amount %20of %20work

Chapter 5

Successful Examples from Experience That Illustrate Improvements

Examples from experience will be presented that demonstrate potential benefits from ethical leadership. These benefits include:

1. Improvements in productivity and efficiency
2. Machine downtime reduction
3. Reductions in the number of accidents and injuries
4. Increases in customer satisfaction
5. Reductions in Work in Progress (WIP)
6. Reductions in Raw Material inventory
7. Increase in throughput
8. Reductions in utility costs
9. Avoidance of penalties and fine due to mismanagement of resources and working conditions

These examples were successful due to the ethical leadership provided by all levels of management before, during, and after the changes were made. This leadership required the ethical collection, reporting, and analysis of data and information and the use of critical thinking to minimize the probability of making a mistake. Employee engagement was enhanced due to the involvement of effected employees before, during, and after the change was made. Based on many years of experience, employees will continue to

DOI: 10.4324/9781003302308-5

initiate improvements if supported by management and given the opportunities and support.

5.1 The Relocation of a Workstation to Reduce the Excessive Motion of an Employee with a Leg Brace

After a material handler moved a chair from the elevator and placed it immediately behind the workstation, the hand sand operater lifted the frame manually approximately 15 inches onto the workstation, grasped a hand sander that was operated pneumatically, sanded the frame as needed, lowered the frame onto the wooden floor, and pushed it to the inspection station which was located adjacent to the paint line. The distance the frame was moved varied with the location of the sanding booth, As seen in Figure 5.1, the booths were aligned on two sides of the department.

During the mapping of the flow of product through the plant, the author noticed one operator, currently assigned to booth two, was wearing a brace on her ankle due to a recent accident. This operator was manually moving a completed chair across an uneven wooden concrete floor in excess of 100 feet to the quality inspection workstation with a brace on her right foot.

The author noticed that workstation two was not currently in use and advised the supervisor who immediately relocated that operator to the vacant booth. This move was possible since each booth was identical except for location. The author arranged a meeting with the plant manager and maintenance to suggest further improvements. An air-assist lift table operated by a foot pedal was installed to eliminate the lifting and subsequent lowering of the chair. These tables reduced the risk of injury due to strain. Additionally, the hand sander used by the operator was evaluated for a potential replacement to reduce possible injury due to constant vibration. The vendor of the sandpaper was called to determine potential replacements. Due to a longstanding relationship with the vendor, a newer, more ergonomic model was provided at no charge provided that they remain as vendor.

TITLE		Sanding Booth (plan view)					
Figure Number		5.1	Drawn By	JD	Date	10/4/2020	
Sanding Department							
Checked by	JW	Date	3/1/2021	ECO #	978-024		

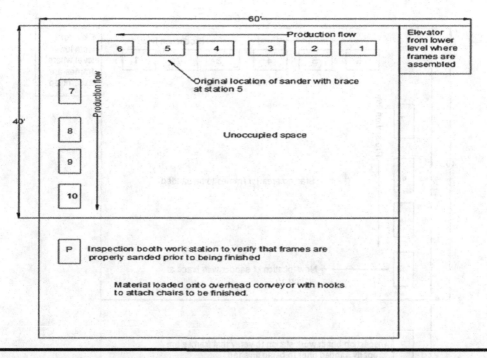

Figure 5.1 A hand sanding department with identical workstations with the location of an operator with a brace on one leg.

Cost justification for the purchase and installation of the lift tables was not possible due to the lack of detailed time studies for the hand sanding process. The installation was performed due to the recommendation of the safety team and to increase employee engagement (Figure 5.2).

TITLE	Sanding Booth (plan view)					
Figure Number		5.2	Drawn By	JD	Date	10/4/2020
Sanding Department						
Checked by	JW	Date	3/1/2021	ECO #	978-024	

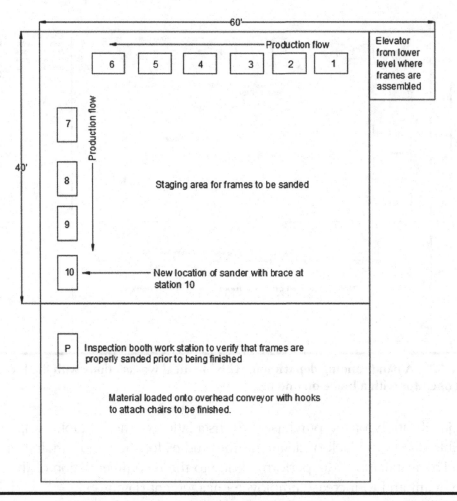

Figure 5.2   A hand sanding department with identical workstations after the relocation of an operator with a brace on one leg.

5.2 An Improvement Due to Increasing the Length of a Hose Line Dispensing Gasoline

The author was waiting in line to fuel his vehicle, as depicted in Figure 5.3. Due to the length of hoses, automobiles could only be serviced on the side of the pump that corresponded to the side of the vehicle containing the fuel tank.

TITLE	Fueling Station (plan view)				
Figure Number	5.3	Drawn By	JD	Date	10/15/2020
Fueling Station					
Checked by	JW	Date	3/15/2021	ECO #	978-026	

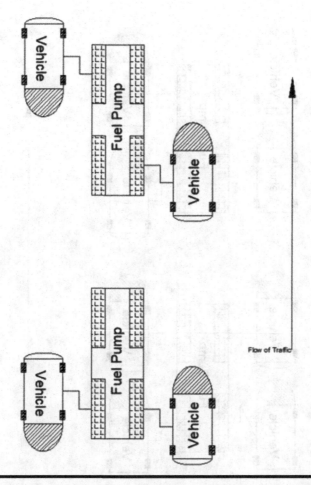

Figure 5.3   Queued vehicles awaiting available open pump before lengthening of hoses.

The author realized that if vehicles could receive service on either side of the pump regardless of the location of the fuel tank, the customer would realize reduced wait time and the provider would increase resource utilization and customer satisfaction which should result in improved sales and profit. After the author discussed this opportunity with management, the following changes were made as can be seen in Figure 5.4.

TITLE	Fueling Station (plan view)					
Figure Number		5.4	Drawn By	JD	Date	10/15/2020
Fueling Station						
Checked by	JW	Date	3/15/2021	ECO #	978-026	

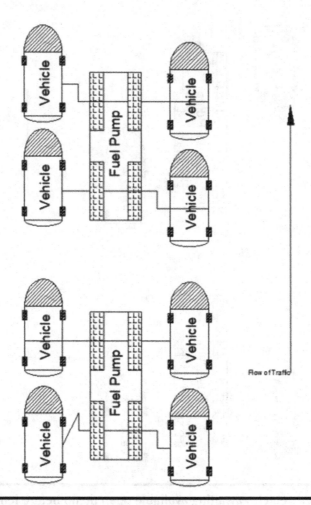

Figure 5.4 Queued vehicles awaiting available open pump after lengthening of hoses.

5.3 Improvements Due to Workplace Redesign in an Automobile Dealership

This example occurred in an automobile dealership. This change was implemented successfully due to value stream mapping resulting in increased productivity, income for the technicians and dealership, customer relations, and ethical behavior.

The existing process of oil and filter changes at an automobile dealership:

1. The technicians would walk the parking area to locate a car to be serviced as the result of a lack of scheduling the process of an oil and filter change.

2. The technician would then drive the car to be serviced into the facility and onto the rack.

3. The technician would then walk approximately 50 feet to the parts department to request the number of quarts of oil needed and an oil filter.

4. Upon availability of the parts technician, he would determine the correct oil filter, remove it, walk to the second floor where cases of different brands and viscosities of oil were located, get a brand of oil with the specified viscosity, return to the parts department, and provide the supplies to the technician to enable the customer to be charged for the supplies.

5. The parts department technician would then list the parts supplied on a lined pad. The lines were then cut by a paper cutter, manually sorted by part category, and the count of each item would then be deducted from the existing inventory.

6. The automobile technician would return to his workstation, perform the services as specified, sign the work order verifying the completion of the work, that the work had been done, turn a copy to the office, return the car to any available space, and locate another car awaiting service and repeat the process.

Analysis of process:

The author performed an analysis of the usage of filters and discovered that over 80% of the filter changes involved only three different filters. The number of different oil filters in inventory exceeded 20. The results of a simple time study taken for further analysis revealed the time that the technician consumed to go to the parts room, wait for the parts, return to his workstation, and the time for the parts technician to service the car and locate the next car in the queue.

Modifications that resulted from the analysis:

1. Flow-through racks containing two brands of motor oil with the same viscosity were installed in front of each oil changing station.

2. Racks containing the most used oil filters were placed in front of each oil changing station. Signs were placed in front of each filter indicating the brand and year that required that particular filter.

3. Kan-Ban cards were also placed in front of each type of filter and brand of oil. As the technician removed a filter and oil, he compared the remaining quantity of each item with the remaining in the racks and if

either quantity equaled or was less than the reorder point on the green kan-ban card. The technician took the card to the parts technician to the parts department clerk who entered an order for the needed parts.

The process after methods improvement:

1. The technician locates a car to be serviced by looking at the dashboard of cars parked on the side of the dealership.
2. The technician, after driving the car to be serviced into the shop onto the lift, obtains the correct filter from the rack, the number of quarts of oil needed, and services the car.
3. The technician completes the work order verifying that the work had been done, signs it, and submits the signed work order to the office, returns the car to an available space, and locates another car awaiting service.

Process steps eliminated:

1. The automobile technician traveling to the parts department and returning.
2. The parts technician writing down each individual order from the automobile technician and retrieving the parts from the needed locations.

Opportunities for further improvement:

1. The assignment of completing repair orders for oil and filter changes to one service order technician to improve this process. Currently, there were four service order technicians who could complete work orders, resulting in the likelihood of more work orders for oil and filter changes than could be completed.
2. A scheduling system to inform each automobile technician of the location of the next automobile to be serviced and a service sequence based on first in first out.
3. A system to evaluate the productivity of each automobile technician.

The reasons for the success of this improvement were that the author developed a process map and took a simple time study to document the time spent performing each of these activities. The author made a presentation to management to demonstrate the amount of time they consumed performing unnecessary tasks and the excessive inventory.

5.4 An Improvement Due to the Addition of a Work Cell in the Metal Fabrication Department of a Furniture Plant

A value stream map of the flow of raw material through a metal frame component in the metal fabrication department revealed that individual independent processes could be replaced with a manufacturing cell. Prior to the installation of the work cell, each process was initiated by a work order and consisted of a material handler bringing material to be processed in a tote bin, a rectangular-sided container designed to be used with a forklift, an operator removing the material, performing the operation as needed, and aiding the completed component into another tote bin that was transported to the next process. There were six processes needed to fabricate the component in preparation for painting.

The manufacturing cell can be seen in Figure 5.5. The use of the cell reduced the number of manufacturing orders from six to one, simplified the bill of material and process routing, reduced the floor space needed in the metal fabrication department by 40%. The direct labor saved by not having to load and unload each machine was replaced by increased inspection due to the installation of a check fixture located as the last process in the cell.

TITLE	Manufacturing Cell (plan view)					
Figure Number		5.5	Drawn By	JD	Date	10/1/2020
Manufacturing Cell						
Checked by	JW	Date	2/24/2021	ECO #	978-023	

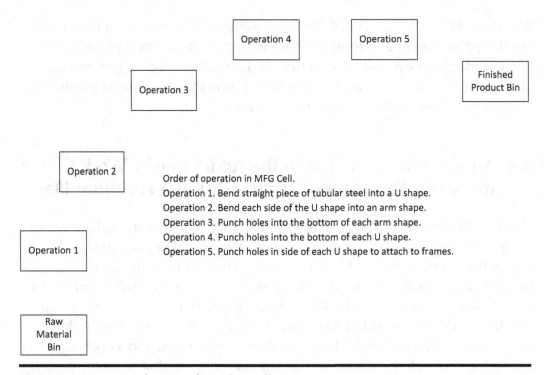

Figure 5.5   Layout of a manufacturing cell.

5.5 An Improvement Due to the Relocation of a Refrigerator in a Public Health Department

The author observed in a public health department that clients waited in line for a variety of services to be seen by an incoming clerk. The clerk would obtain the needed information and provide directions as needed to the appropriate clinic. The only exception to this procedure occurred if the client requested a vaccination. In this situation, the clerk would walk with the patient down the hall and set the client on a bench to wait until the technician was available to administer the requested vaccination. The current setup can be seen in Figure 5.6.

TITLE	Injection Area (plan view)					
Figure Number	5.6	Drawn By	JD	Date	10/7/2020	
Injection Area						
Checked by	JW	Date	3/10/2021	ECO #	978-025	

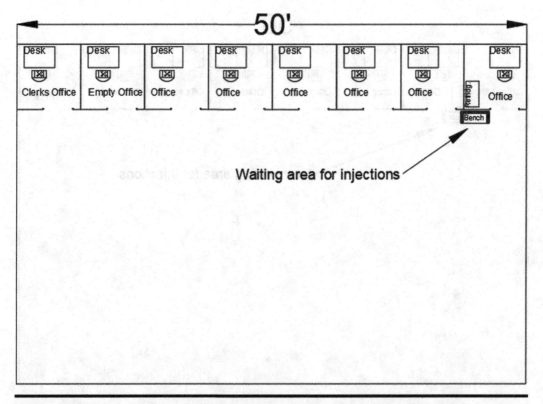

Figure 5.6   Layout of the health department clinic to demonstrate the distance that the clerk must travel to accompany patients who need vaccinations.

The author noticed that although an empty office was adjacent to the clerk's desk, the clerk and client walked to the end of the hall. When asked why this occurred, the response was that the last office contained a refrigerator and that the vaccines needed to be refrigerated to maintain their efficacy. The author examined the refrigerator and realized that it was a household model that used 110 volts. The author then asked if the refrigerator could be moved into the vacant office. The relocation of the refrigerator would reduce the unnecessary travel time for the clerk and clients and provide additional time for the clerk to service clients. The close proximity would reduce the likelihood of the compromise of personal information.

The changes can be seen in Figure 5.7.

TITLE	Injection Area (plan view)						
Figure Number		5.7	Drawn By	JD		Date	10/7/2020
Injection Area							
Checked by	JW	Date	3/10/2021		ECO #	978-025	

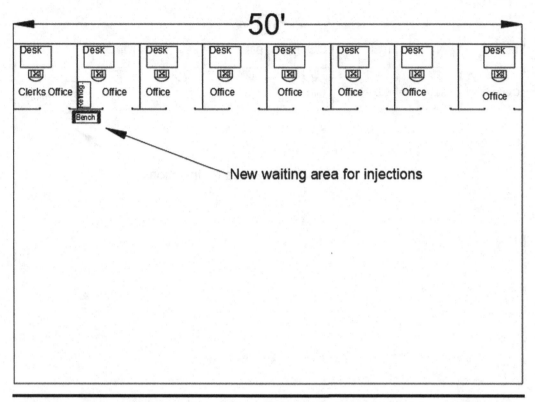

New waiting area for injections

Figure 5.7   Layout of the health department after the relocation of the office that administered vaccines.

5.6 Improvement Due to the Relocation of a Sewing Department in a Furniture Plant

As the author was touring a furniture plant on his first day of employment, he noticed that the sewing department was not located adjacent to the upholstery department. It was centered in a different department that was approximately one-fourth of a mile distant. This required that sewn covers be loaded into laundry baskets which were then loaded into a small van to be delivered to the upholstery department. The operators in the sewing department were paid on an incentive system that required that each sewn cover be manually counted by a material handler before the cover could be carried to the upholstery department. After the truck was docked at the upholstery department and the laundry baskets removed, the sewn covers were recounted by a different material handler before being given to an upholster.

The author asked management why was the sewing department in the current location. The author was advised that the sewing department was in its current location due to a lack of parking space near the upholstery department. The author contacted a contractor for an estimate to add sufficient parking spaces near the upholstery department and compared those costs with the savings that would result from the elimination of the truck and driver. The author calculated the payback, which was less than one year. Management authorized the project. One requirement that the author required prior to the implementation of the project was that any displaced employee would be transferred to an equal-paying position.

5.7 An Example That Resulted in Reduced Motion of Indirect Labor in a Furniture Plant

Another opportunity to reduce waste and excessive motion existed in the same plant.

Foam was received and stored in racks with three shelves high. The receiving crew consisted of three people who, based on work sampling studies, spent two hours a day removing foam from the trailer, placing it into the assigned storage location, and scanning each piece to the raw material inventory. Larger and bulkier pieces of foam were placed on the lower racks and the smaller and less bulky pieces were on the upper racks. Safety rules required that two material handlers were needed when a ladder was used, one to handle the foam and one to hold the ladder. A different crew of three would remove the foam from its stored location and transport it to an upholstery cell when needed. From the various methods available to determine the length of time required for these two tasks, to unload and store a truckload (T/L) of foam in the proper load and then to remove the foam from the assigned location to the designated workstation, the author selected work sampling for the following reasons:

1. The variability in assigned storage locations: some foam kits were assigned the bottom row, as kits for sofas, due to their size and bulkiness; others were assigned locations on the top of shelves which required the use of a ladder and two material handlers.
2. The variability in the size and quantity of items of each foam kit: some kits contained only one item, as kits for chairs that had a wooden back; some for sofas and wing chairs had multiple pieces that were tied together.
3. The variability in the distance from the assigned area of the foam kit to the designated workstation: kits with the greatest usage were assigned areas that were closest to the production areas.

The author then conducted multiple work sampling studies indicating that the crew of three spent two hours per day performing this task, which equaled the time needed to unload the foam from the vendor and place it into the correct location.

The company employed material requirements planning (MRP) to ensure that inventory was available when needed to prevent stock-outs, which would result in the cessation of production or at the very minimum a change in the schedule to produce according to available inventory and not per the schedule. Possible late deliveries could result from rescheduling orders. The author observed on several occasions one crew removing foam from the vendor and storing it in the proper location and a different crew removing foam from the same location and transporting it to an upholstery cell.

The author presented management with this improvement opportunity to determine a solution. A meeting was held with production, purchasing, and the vendor, and the decision was made to install Just-in-Time (JIT) manufacturing. The result of this installation would enable the receiving crew to remove the foam from the vendor's trailer and take it directly to the designated upholstery cell. Purchasing coordinated with production to determine

Figure 5.8   Picture of chair with multiple unique foam pieces [1].

how the trailer would be loaded so that the first item loaded was the first item needed in production and the last item remaining on the trailer was the last item needed for production.

This change resulted in increased productivity due to the elimination of double handling of the foam which enabled the reassignment of three members to other departments. Savings also resulted from a reduction of warehouse storage needed for raw material and the potential of damaged foam due to less handling.

5.8 Improvement Due to the Installation of MRP in a Furniture Plant That Manufactured Modular Kitchen Cabinets and Bathroom Vanities

The author worked for a company that manufactured modular kitchen cabinets, base and wall units, and bathroom vanities. The minimum width of base cabinets was 9 inches and the maximum 96 and was available in increments of 3 inches. The height of all base cabinets was identical. The wall cabinets varied in both width and height: the narrowest was 9 inches and the widest was 96 inches; the minimum height was 12 inches and the maximum was 36 inches. As a result, the number of combinations of height and width was numerous.

In addition, each base cabinet was available in four different styles and four different stains so the total number of different base cabinets that was available was now multiplied by a factor of 16. The different number of vanity cabinets was somewhat less since this product was limited to base units. A base unit sits on the floor and a wall unit is mounted on a wall. As a result, the total number of different available products was huge.

In this situation items with different manufacturing dates were subject to color variations in the stains. The company manufactured and shipped products throughout the US. Cabinets that were installed in close proximately with color variations resulted in numerous complaints. The color variations were due to variations in manufacturing dates.

The author worked for this company before military service and again at the completion of his service. During that period the company installed an MRP system that enabled the company to produce not only those items that had been ordered but enabled a complete order to be stained at one time. This not only reduced the production of items that had not been ordered but also complaints due to stain variations.

Productivity increased as a result of not manufacturing products that remained in a warehouse waiting for an order and fewer complaints due to color variation. Implementation of the MRP system was responsible for the increase in material and labor utilization.

5.9 Improvement Due to the Elimination of a Process in a Paper Converting Plant

The author worked for a paper converter that manufactured paper tubes for the textile and carpet industry. If a customer ordered a carpet-grade tube with a length of 50 inches, the machine would produce a tube that was 152 inches in length, allowing for waste, and bundle them with 19 to a bundle and transport them to the re-cutting department and place them into an empty bundling rack (Figure 5.9).

TITLE	Fixture for racking tubes manually (orthogonal view)					
Figure Number		5.9	Drawn By	JD	Date	7/25/2020
Fixture for racking tubes manually						
Checked By	JW	Date	1/22/2021	ECO #	978-005	

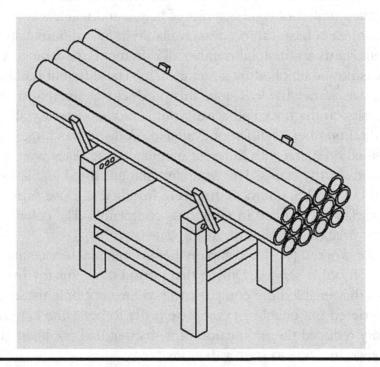

Figure 5.9   Fixture for racking tubes manually that can be adjusted for various outside diameters of tubes (orthogonal view).

TITLE	Fixture for racking tubes manually (plan, top, and right-hand side views)						
Figure Number		5.10	Drawn By		JD	Date	7/25/2020
Fixture for racking tubes manually							
Checked By		JW	Date	1/22/2021		ECO #	978-005

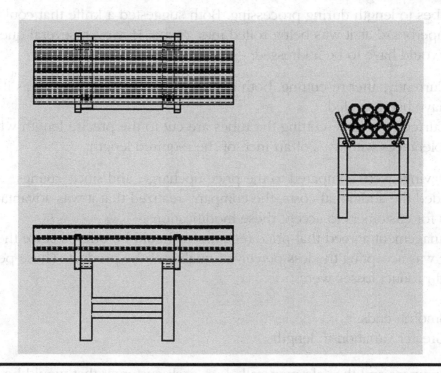

Figure 5.10   Fixture for racking tubes manually that can be adjusted for various outside diameters of tubes (plan, top, and right-hand side views).

This department consisted of one re-cutter operated by one operator. This operator cut the bundle with steel band cutters (Figure 5.10). The operator would pick up one tube from the rack and slide the tube to be cut onto the mandrel, which was 36 inches high to the center of the mandrel; cut one inch off one end by depressing the foot pedal and disposing of the waste into an adjacent carton; move the remainder of the tube to the designated stop position that was adjustable (for this order it was set at 50 inches – the length of tube ordered); depress a foot pedal which activated the cutter to cut the tube at the required length; grasp the cut tube and place into a bundling rack; return to the re-cutter; and continue this process until the bundling rack contained 19 tubes. The operator would then strap the bundle with three steel straps and wait for a forklift to remove the bundled tubes so that the process can begin. This process continued until all the tubes with the original length had been recut.

Although there was a re-cutting upcharge for this operation, the author realized that the extra operation fell into the category of overprocessing. He began discussing possibilities with management and maintenance for cutting the tubes to length during processing. Both suggested a knife that could cut the paperboard as it was being rolled into a tube. However, several questions would have to be addressed:

1. Currently, after re-cutting, both ends of the tube were smooth as if they have been sanded.
2. Currently, after re-cutting the tubes are cut to the precise length with tolerances within $1/8$ of an inch of the required length.

Cost savings were compared to the price upcharge, and since savings exceeded the additional costs, the company realized that it was advantageous for customers to accept these modifications.

Management agreed that price reductions should be offered since the customer was accepting the less perceived quality of the product. These perceived product losses were:

1. Smooth ends.
2. Greater variation in length.

The engineer and the salesman called on each customer that would be affected by the proposed change. The engineer first explained the current process and discussed the proposed change. The salesman then stated that there would be a cost reduction if the proposed change was acceptable. Every customer without exception understood the need for the change and would have accepted it without the savings but was appreciative of it.

This modification to the manufacturing process succeeded because it asked the critical questions needed and involved those who needed to be: management, maintenance, plant personnel, and the customer.

1. What effect would eliminating the re-cutting operation have on the final product?
   It would eliminate the smooth ends and result in a length variation as much as ½ inch in the final product.

2. Were these variations allowable in the current specifications?
   The current specifications did not mention smooth ends or length tolerances, but these tubes had been delivered to customers over many
   years. Compared to the current product, the customer may have thought
   the new product was of lower quality which is the reason a discount
   was offered.
3. Did the change produce cost savings?
   Direct labor costs decreased from the elimination of the separate re-
   cutting operation.
   Direct labor costs increased from the one additional bundler needed
   when these tubes were being produced.
   The net result was a saving in direct labor costs.
   Costs that need to be determined:

A. Costs of re-cutting per M tubes designated as C(R).
B. Costs of direct labor for the one additional person needed to bundle
   tubes with the new process designated as C(B).
C. Cost of one additional band of steel strap (½ inch × 0.020) used to
   encapsulate tubes designated as C(D).

Sales discount given to accept tubes with less "perceived" quality designated
S(D).

Savings per M could be calculated as C(R) less the sum of C(B), C(S) and
C(D).

5.10 Improvement Due to the Elimination of Waste in a Paper Converting Plant

This reduction was achieved due to a change in the method of application
of latex.

Latex is a type of aqueous adhesive that is non-toxic and odorless. It
has numerous applications as in the manufacture of furniture, now-woven
fabrics, paper processing, and wireless binding. Characteristics include
excellent initial tackiness, a shelf life of one year, and without harmful
materials [2].

The change involved the installation of an electric eye that would detect
the beginning of the paper tube as it was extruded from the mandrel. A
spray gun would spray a controlled amount of latex onto the tube at the

beginning of the extrusion process and stop when the tube completely left the mandrel. This change not only reduced the cost of the latex but eliminated the need to elevate the five-gallon bucket onto the stand four feet high and the inserting of a slot ¼ inch × 1 inch into the bottom and insured that correct alignment onto the tube. Also, the amount of latex that did not flow onto tubes but rather flowed onto the floor into the waiting drain that fed into the local sewer system was greatly reduced.

This discussion resulted in an example of a successful change in the manufacturing process that involved the application of latex adhesive on the outside of a paper tube. The latex was purchased in five-gallon buckets and applied to the outside of paper tubes to provide an adhesive surface to grab a material to initiate the wrapping process. It was applied by having the bucket mounted in a metal stand over the tube as it was removed from the machine by the drilling of a slot in the bottom of the bucket that provided a continuous flow of the latex. Tubes were produced continually, but since the length of the tubes varied, there was a gap between tubes that varied as the length of tubes. Since the flow of the latex was continuous, some of the latex flowed onto tubes but some was wasted and flowed into a drain and ultimately the local water supply.

The manufacturing process consists of installing a roll of paperboard into a stand, feeding the roll through a section of rollers that applies adhesive and maintains a constant pressure, then cutting the paperboard to the specified length by the activation of a knife as the paperboard triggers an electric eye which is located above the mandrel. A carriage transports the length into a slit in a mandrel that becomes the diameter of the tube, is rolled into a tube as the mandrel is rotated in a counterclockwise direction, and the recently wound tube is removed from the mandrel by an arm attached to the end of the carriage onto a conveyor belt that conveys the tubes into an oven to dry the adhesive.

The production rate as measured by tubes per minute was limited by the carriage and did not vary with the length of the tube but did vary inversely with the width of the paperboard used to manufacture the tube due to having less control with a wider sheet.

The production standard was not based on the length of the tube. Frequency of roll changes varied inversely with the tube length. A production standard did exist for roll changes, which varied directly with the width of the roll to be installed on a pneumatic stand.

The industrial engineering technician who calculated productivity daily was also given the additional task of determining the total number of linear inches of tubes produced each day, making sure to include the waste attributable to the latex application broken down by the thickness of the tube to ascertain waste varied by thickness. The amount of waste generated during manufacturing and the number of defects was decomposed by length, and the percentage did not vary with the length of the tube.

The critical questions that were asked that resulted in this being a successful application were:

1. What other methods exist for applying latex?

   The team investigated three methods: brushing, application with a roller or similar device, and spraying. Due to the curvature of the surface, the need for consistency in the amount applied, and the ability to control the amount applied by order, the use of a pneumatic spray gun option was chosen because it was the easiest one to install and maintain. This option was selected.

2. Will additional manpower be needed?

   The existing crew consisted of three people: an operator, an assistant, and a bundler. The bundler assisted during setups and roll changes as did the assistant operator. Tasks associated with changeovers included relocating an electric eye that determines the length of the tube. The new method involved two additional electric eyes, one placed at the beginning of the disposal of the tube from the mandrel and the other at the discharge end. The relocation of these two electric eyes would require no more than one minute and could be easily added to the existing tasks of the existing crew.

3. What will be the installation cost for this new method?

   Conversion to this new process required the purchase and installation of an additional electric eye and spray equipment that could easily pump latex from the bucket it was purchased into the spray gun. As the tube was removed from the mandrel, the electric eye activated the spray gun and deactivated it as the tube left the mandrel.

   Inventories of pneumatic hoses were maintained due to normal deterioration as were air guns. Allocation of maintenance hours to projects or machines was not kept, so the determination of the cost of installation cost was not possible in this situation. An estimate of $2,000 was used, which was known to be excessive. As a rule of thumb, if unsure of estimating, always estimate costs to be greater than expected, since it is always better to have the project realize savings greater than expected rather than less than expected. Always use the exact cost from quotes if available.

4. What are the savings for this new method?
    A. The first step to calculate savings required the usage of latex per (thousand per linear inch of tube) MLI of quality tubes produced by each method of application- the current method of dripping the latex versus spraying the latex.
    B. A. The engineering technician maintained the inventory level of latex in addition to calculating the usage per MLI for each application method.
    C. The latex costs MLI for each method of application was determined by multiplying the cost per pound of latex by the difference is usage between the two methods of application. The costs of the latex included inbound freight.
    D. The cost savings per period was computed by the engineering technician by multiplying the lowest cost of application by the MLI of quality tubes produced during that period.

5. What effect will changing the method of latex application have on the process of manufacturing paper tubes?
    The question was asked to crew members and management and the unanimous answer was that there would be no effect. This was confirmed by the author with random sampling studies and relatedly constant productivity and efficiency percentages.

6. What is the revenue earned from the latex?
    The industrial engineering technician calculated the revenue from the upcharge for several months after the change. The revenue earned was compared with the cost of latex consumed during the same period and this project was very cost effective.
    It is crucial after the conclusion of a project to compare the savings gained or additional revenue earned to the cost of the project for several reasons:
    A. To validate the costs and savings as depicted in the project proposal.
    B. To learn and gain experience to enhance project management.

7. How will this affect the purchasing of the raw material?
   The purchasing agent stated that after the project was completed the frequency of purchases would be reduced.
8. Will additional training be required for the machine operator?
   The maintenance department discussed in detail the operation of the spray system with all members of the crew and demonstrated the air pressure required, and fully trained all members of the crew on each shift in its operation.

5.11 A Suggested Improvement Due to Inventory Reduction of Finished Goods in a Plant That Manufactured Woven Labels

The author worked in a plant that manufactured printed labels on narrow fabric. These labels were sewn into garments and contained information about the proper care for the item to which the label was sewn as well as the size of the garment. The manufacturing of these labels required many processes including the winding of yarn onto a beam, the weaving of the narrow fabric, the coating of the fabric with starch to stiffen the fabric, the printing of the label onto the fabric, and the cutting, folding, and packaging of the label. All labels were packaged 1M (thousand) per carton to simplify the process of taking physical inventory. Since labels were priced per million, training was an continual process to prevent errors in shipping and the quantities to be produced.

Major customers included manufacturers of tee shirts, underwear, and most other outerwear.

Due to the inability to accurately predict sales by item, the major customers requested that a minimum level of inventory of each label be maintained for immediate shipment upon issuing an order. The manufacturer of the labels agreed since the company guaranteed that any label would be in any customer's plant regardless of location within five working days after receipt of the order. Frequently orders were produced and packaged using overtime in order to maintain this level of inventory. This inventory was maintained without a memo of understanding or other documents that a vendor would purchase existing inventory before initiating changes that would obsolete a particular label. Numerous customers had many different labels that were changed frequently due to the variety of products and several labels contained an inventory of millions of labels. Those labels that were replaced with an updated version became obsolete but remained in the finished goods inventory just in case the label was needed in the future by that customer.

Because the author had witnessed on several occasions employees working overtime to produce and package labels that was placed in finished goods inventory instead of being shipped and due to his experience with inventory reduction and JIT manufacturing, he proposed to upper management various strategies that would reduce finished goods inventory. He used those incidents in which he observed employees working overtime at a higher rate to fill finished goods warehouse locations as a foundation for his presentation. He emphasized that implementing those strategies would yield many benefits including a reduction in direct labor costs.

Although the director of manufacturing and the manager of customer service agreed that a majority of orders could be produced and shipped in less time than the lead time given by the customer, they were uncomfortable with the concept and did not agree to implement any of the strategies proposed by the author even on a temporary basis. Soon after the negative response, the author obtained another position and the company shutdown due to their customers printing labels directly onto garments which eliminated the need for the purchased label.

5.12 An Example of Improvement Due to the Quick Exchange of Dies in the Metal Fabrication Department of a Furniture Plant

The quick exchange of dies, forms, etc. reduces the amount of time needed to exchange a die, form, etc. and increases the time available for manufacturing quality products. One team on which the author worked was a maintenance team with a furniture company. The company produced metal frame dinette suites and used a 150-ton press to produce the plate used to attach the swivel assembly onto the chair frame. The maintenance team documented the current steps to change the die in the press. These steps consisted of the following:

1. Upon notification that a change needed to be made, obtain and place some tools onto a golf cart.
2. Drive a golf cart to the metal fabrication department that contained the press.

3. Stop at the break area for coffee since the break area was en route.
4. Arrive at the press to be changed and realize that the needed tools were not on the golf cart.
5. Return to the maintenance area and select the correct tools.
6. Stop at the break area for coffee since the break area was en route.
7. Arrive at the press and initiate the change.
8. Verify with the supervisor that the press with the changed die produced quality components.
9. Stop at the break area for coffee since the break area was en route to the maintenance department.
10. Plug the golf cart into the recharger.
11. The average overall time for a die change was approximately eight hours.

During the discussion, the maintenance department realized that there were two dies that were used in that press. The planning department mentioned each plate required a different raw material that differed in width which was received in rolls. The planning department during the meeting stated that the two plates produced by this press were not scheduled by MRP but in batches based on the number of mounting plates that each roll could produce. This was done to reduce the frequency of roll changes due to the time needed to change rolls. Each die required a different width of material.

The improvement team included members from maintenance, the planning department, the press operator, the plant engineer, and the supervisor of the assembly department. The first item discussed was to assign an approximate time for each main task. Then the team proposed solutions for each task. The plant engineer proposed a slight redesign of the die that would enable removal of the die from the press and the repositioning of the new die in the press with the use of a forklift. The use of a forklift eliminated the use of a bulky overhead mounted hoist.

This modification was agreed to by all team members. The team then suggested to maintenance that two separate tool kits be assembled and identified by the width of the raw material. Coupled with this suggestion was that the supervisor would inform maintenance of an impending need to change the die, the approximate time that the change would occur, and identify the width of the new raw material.

The notification enable maintenance to load the correct tool kit onto the golf cart and arrive at the press prepared for the change. The improvements recommended by this continuous improvement team and implemented resulted in the following improvements:

1. A drastic reduction in change over time on this press, from a mean time of eight hours to one of two hours or a reduction of 75 percent.
2. An increase in manufacturing throughput.
3. A reduction in indirect labor costs.

References

1. Image of Upholstered Chair with multiple pieces of foam. Retreived 3/31/2023 from: https://www.bing.com/images/search?view=detailV2&ccid=GLrxwAVn&id=718CAAAC74806FD8DB38A1194FC4C 32639E89856&thid=OIP.GLrxwAVngB VjY0J6dinoVAHaHy&mediaurl=https %3a%2f%2f3.bp.blogspot.com%2f -kLt51nbY-3Y%2fUgRIV7twkFI% 2fAAAAAAAAE7E%2fRMkyuIk8UV0% 2fs1600% 2fIMG_1871.JPG&cdnurl=https%3a%2f%2fth.bing.com%2fth%2fid%2f R.18baf1c0056780156363427a7629e854%3frik%3dVpjoOSbDxE8ZoQ%26pid% 3dImgRaw%26r%3d0&exph=1600&expw=1521&q=Free+Image+Of +Upholstered+Chair&simid=608001669762926800&FORM=IRPRST&ck=CDE41C E170D86A66303A45E296F0C63E&selectedIndex=0&idpp=overlayview&ajaxhist =0&ajaxserp=0
2. White latex adhesive. (n.d.). Retrieved 2/20/2021 from: http://www.hhsj.chem-china.com/gzsjen/index.htm

Index

Printed in the United States
by Baker & Taylor Publisher Services